Ecology
FOR BEGINNERS

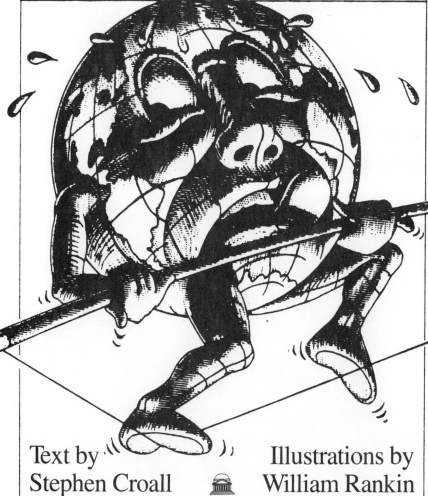

Text by
Stephen Croall

Illustrations by
William Rankin

Pantheon Books, New York

3

Library of Congress Cataloging in Publication Data

Croall, Stephen.
Ecology for beginners.

1. Human ecology.   I. Rankin, William.   II. Title.
GF41.C76   304.2   81-47191
ISBN 0-394-74872-7   AACR2

Manufactured in the United States of America

9 8 7 6 5 4 3

About the Author and Illustrator

Stephen Croall is a British writer and journalist currently living on a farm in Sweden. A former Reuter correspondent in Stockholm and London, he has also worked as a musician, a shoemaker, and a day-nursery apprentice. He is the author of *The Anti-Nuclear Handbook*.

William Rankin is a British designer and illustrator based in Stockholm.

ecology (eekoloji) *n* – study of relations of living organisms to their environment; study of ecosystems; study of the environmental conditions of existence.

The story so far . . .

Planet Earth condensed 4,600 million years ago from hot gases and cosmic dust. It cooled into a beautiful blue orb, slightly squashed at one pole but still easy to fall in love with. Barring accidents, like the sun going out, it will be here for another 10,000 million years.

It may seem big to us but Earth is a tiny speck in a universe so huge that your brain hurts just thinking about it.

But where on earth did the universe come from?

Life

commercial
An Artist's Impression of the Arrival of the First Organisms

The first organisms lived on sulphur . . .

Then some of them began giving off oxygen and the air-breathers inherited the Earth . . .

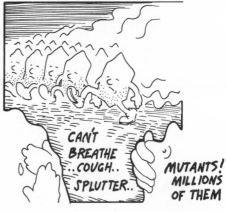

These bacteria gave off 'waste' that in time became fossil and mineral deposits. Some bacteria evolved into plants while others chose to become animals.

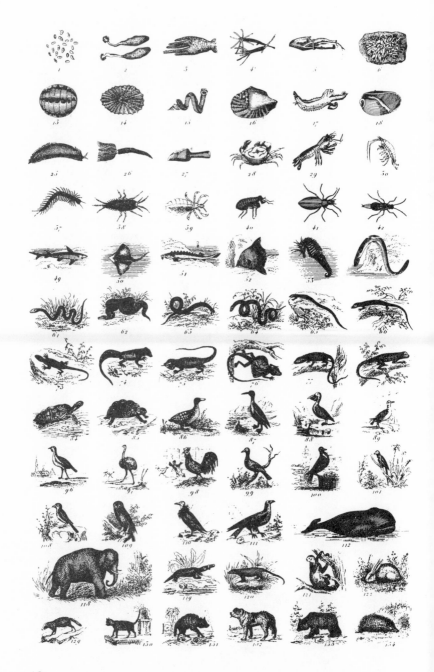

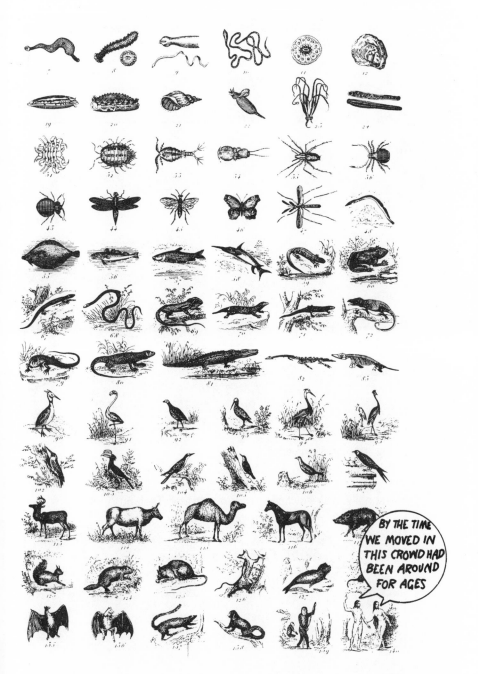

11

Imagining the history of the Earth as one month,* human beings in their present form (*homo sapiens*) have only been here …

* 1 day = 150 million years

Personally, we're inclined to agree with Mao Tsetung …

Early Man and Woman behaved themselves quite well.

The world had only five or ten million inhabitants in those days so there was plenty of elbow-room. They hunted, slashed-and-burned, fished, gathered, and ate each other for 99% of human history.

The Neolithic Revolution

SEVEN seconds ago on our historical calendar a lot of people tired of chasing about being good ecologists. They started putting down roots.

ONE FINE SPRING MORN

LET'S BE MOVING ON

HANG ON WHILE I STORE ME NUTS

JEDDAH 9,632 BC

MEANWHILE...

SOME MOONS LATER

WOW!

WHAT'S ALL THIS THEN?

LOOKS LIKE THE BIRTH OF AGRICULTURE TO ME

MAYBE WE SHOULD SETTLE DOWN?

GOOD IDEA. WE'RE FRESH OUT OF TENT PEGS

THE TAMING OF THE OATS

DOMESTICATION CON'T

WHAT'S YOUR NAME?

WOLF, WOLF!

AGAIN!

WOOF WOOF!

INUES APACE

CHEEP CHEEP?

SHIP?.. ER..UM.. ..SHOP?.. .ER...

The invention of agriculture was a turning point in human history. The hunters and nomadic herdsmen became 'marginal' and only survived in places that no-one else wanted: the African bush, the Australian outback, the arctic regions of America and Siberia, etc.

They had left nature largely undisturbed. The peasants who succeeded them shaped the environment, integrating themselves with nature. They intervened directly in the *ecosystem*.

The Ecosystem

The ecosystem is the complex web linking animals, plants, air, water and every other lifeform in the biosphere. It all hangs together. The system is in a 'steady state' of dynamic balance, which means that by altering any one part you affect all the others.

Humans are only one factor in the ecosystem. But we don't quite see it that way. We set ourselves apart and call all the other factors or species *natural resources* – or simply *nature*.

← asset hound

Human survival depends upon preserving the ecosystem. It's the boundary of existence, the framework of human activity. The ecosystem can do without us but we can't do without the ecosystem. As long as we live on Earth.

Viewing nature as no more than a bundle of resources for human consumption is inviting trouble.

Commoner's Laws of Ecology:
1. Everything is connected with everything else.
2. Everything must go somewhere.
3. Nature knows best.
4. There's no such thing as a free lunch.

Civilisation

Agriculture spread from southern
Asia and the Middle East
throughout the Eurasian and
African continents, and through
the Americas from Mexico and
northern South America.

People swapped the wandering
life for a roof over their heads,
tilled the soil and kept animals.
Peasants traded surpluses.
Temporary markets became
permanent settlements . . . which
grew . . . and grew . . . and the real
problems began.

and now follows A Disastrous History of Ecology

IN A SOCIAL SETTING

Big urban centres demanded food, fuel and timber. Lots of it. Pressure on the peasants built up and consequently land-care often went out of the window. Nature was abused and misused.

Civilisations collapse

Ecosystems are self-healing – but only up to a point. Failure to take this point felled many a grand culture over the centuries.

The Bible blamed it on God's wrath. Similar floods created similar myths in the Americas, Polynesia and India.

20

Breaches of the Eco-Code would in time cut spectacular swathes of erosion through China. While in Indochina . . .

Of course these were mere primitive societies compared with the Greeks & Romans.

OK, social justice wasn't their hallmark. But surely they understood that soil is the great bridge between the inanimate and the living?

While the First Democracy's soil was blowing into the sea the First Republic was building the first city of a million inhabitants – and the world's biggest sewer.

Brilliant Roman engineering carried human waste out of sight . . . but just dumped it in waterways on the outskirts. At the same time burial consisted of tossing bodies into open pits ringing the city.

Rome became a stinking metropolis, ravaged by plague, and in the words of one historian *"recorded a low point in sanitation and hygiene that more primitive communities never descended to".*

The Romans had other ways of killing themselves. To avoid copper poisoning they made their eating and drinking vessels out of lead.

The Christians decided that nature had no reason for existence but to serve humanity.

Enough Christians remained uneaten to start the Church – and put a stop to the widespread belief that every tree, stream, hill or any other natural object had its own guardian spirit. The Church destroyed this ungodly 'animism' so thoroughly that by the Middle Ages there weren't many trees left in Europe.

ST. FRANCIS

Christian radical. Preached equality of all species in the biosphere. Booted out of the Church. Proclaimed Patron Saint of Ecology by the Pope in 1980.

In the city the air was thickening. Edward I of England decided that execution was the solution to pollution.

SO HOW DO WE KEEP WARM?

WE COULD BURN RATS

On Payne of Death the Burninge of Coal be henceforthe forbydden by law in London Towne that the healthe of the Knights of the Shire may not suffere during theyre resydence herein.

Edward I Rex 1322

Those who didn't freeze to death, choke or hang were treated to the Black Death, an epidemic of bubonic plague that devastated Europe in the 14th century.

WE MAY BE SMALL...

...BUT WE KILLED ONE THIRD OF THE POPULATION

AGRICULTURE WAS RUN DOWN EVERY-WHERE

IT'S GREAT TO BE A WEED THESE DAYS

SKRITCH SCRATCH

The Middle Ages brought science & technology to Europe. They also brought feudal ownership of land by a ruling class of kings & queens, nobles and churchmen. Nature was not the only one being exploited.

Peasants, labourers and craftsfolk were doing all the producing. But who was taking home the winnings?

24

WELL, I HAVE CHURCHES TO BUILD

AND I'VE GOT AN ARMY TO FEED

HUNGRY WORK, SMASHING PEASANT REVOLTS

THERE'S NOT ENOUGH MONEY IN AGRICULTURE

WE MUST BROADEN OUR HORIZONS

NO! I'M AN EAGLE... HONEST

These landowners were more concerned with defending their own positions of power than with such trivia as long-term soil fertility. The merchants who succeeded them couldn't tell an earthworm from an eagle. They were just interested in money. But by the end of the Middle Ages they were getting alarmed.

Spilling out over the map, the European states and their enterprising merchants discovered rich new worlds and turned them into poor ones. Spain and Portugal set the tone, conquering, murdering, looting and enslaving across the globe. While England, France and Holland were messing around in the Indies, the Spanish by mistake 'discovered' America . . .

25

America clearly had to be saved from itself. The place was in a chaotic state. Just listen to an eye-witness account:

" *This is a nation in which there is no kind of commerce, no knowledge of letters, no science of numbers, no title of magistrate or of political superior, no habit of service, riches or poverty, no contracts, no inheritance, no divisions of property, only leisurely occupations, no respect for any kinship but the common ties, no clothes, no agriculture, no metals, no use of corn or wine. The very words denoting lying, treason, deceit, greed, envy, slander and forgiveness have never been heard . . . a sick person is a rare sight.* " Michel de Montaigne

In contrast to these 'savages' the Incas did have agriculture. Describing it, a 20th-century soil expert would say "there has probably never been a system in which agricultural practice and soil organisation were so locked together in a perfect artifact of the mind and spirit". The Conquistadores swiftly wrecked it.

The Spaniards, having ruined much of their own agricultural land by deforestation and overgrazing, introduced both to the New World.

The plucky European
adventurers took home not only
gold and silver bullion but also
more earthy things . . .

Parmentier introduced the
American potato to France by
posting an armed guard round the
potato patch during the day and
withdrawing it at night.

But the new crops that appealed
most to the big powers were those
that provided staple foods and
created the basis for *plantation*
economies . . .

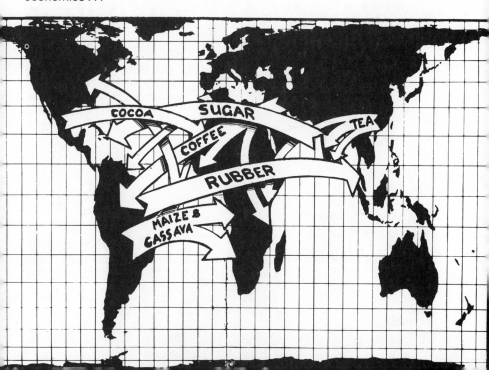

Revolutions

Britain more or less took over in the 18th century. British ships dominated the sea routes and therefore world trade. British capital mounted up. And the British bourgeoisie, the new middle-class rulers, decided the most profitable course would be an Industrial Revolution.

The money was there, thanks to the looting of India, and the machines of mass production were soon invented. But where was the labour?

Scientific, systematic farming with new machines and methods reduced the labour force. Violent and fraudulent land seizures completed the job. Kicked off the land, most peasants had no choice but to become factory fodder – overworked, underpaid and undernourished, reduced from creative workers to 'a mere appendage of flesh on a machine of iron'. They were joined by many craftsfolk whose livelihood had been undercut by machine-made goods.

WANTED DEAD OR ALIVE
for wrecking machinery
and inciting riots

The Art of Housekeeping

Every human society depends for support on a *resource base* (energy and materials).

Primitive communities, slave states and feudal societies relied mainly on *renewable* energy – from the sun, wind, and water – and materials that could be replenished.

They made little lasting impact on nature because their production was restricted by nature's own productivity.

Until capitalism set about industrialising society, nearly 80% of all the things used by humanity came from the animal kingdom and 20% from the mineral kingdom.

Industrialism reversed the trend, concentrating on the Earth's store of *non-renewable* energy and materials, such as fossil fuels and mineral ores.

THE WORD ECOLOGY COMES FROM THE WORD OIKOS

MEANING HOUSE OR HABITAT

The enclosure of common land in Britain signalled the shift from feudalism to capitalism. It also marked the end of a collective view of the resource base and the beginning of a private, egotistical view.

Industrialism switched the emphasis from *reproductive* use of the resource base, which leaves it intact, to *extractive* use, which reduces the total store. Humanity began draining the Earth's 'capital' instead of living off the 'interest'.

FOOLISH HOUSEKEEPING IN ANY HABITAT

OUR HISTORICAL CALENDAR

Industrial capitalism launched the Modern Age, and ripped into the available raw materials with no regard for environmental consequences. By the 19th century Britain had become the 'workshop of the world'.

TECHNOLOGY IS CONQUERING NATURE

RAPE I'D CALL IT

NOWADAYS I'M JUST RAW MATERIAL

AND I'M JUST LABOUR

Having exhausted the supply of fresh trees the industrialists solved the fuel shortage with *fossilised* trees – coal.

OI! TAKE IT EASY. THAT STUFF'S NOT RENEWABLE

MAYBE, BUT I'LL BE DEAD BEFORE IT RUNS OUT

The steam-engine churned. The cotton-mills hummed. The iron industry boomed. New coal-pits were opened. Towns grew into cities and village workshops into factories.

Canals, roads and railway lines criss-crossed the country. Britain throbbed with industrial activity, to quote the school history books. But what else happened?

Industrialism

Factory fumes and waste poisoned the air, water and soil. The chemicals that spewed into the environment hit hardest at the working classes living nearby, often in overcrowded, diseased slums. The factory owners could afford to live away from ugly sights, sounds and smells.

THIS WAS THE SCENE AROUND THE ALKALI FACTORIES

The foul gases, which belch forth night and day from the many factories, rot the clothes, the teeth and in the end the bodies of the workers, and have killed every tree and every blade of grass for miles around.
— Contemporary account

Marx's partner, Friedrich Engels, crossing a Lancashire river, spoke of *"the most disgusting blackish-green slime pools from the depths of which bubbles of miasmatic gas constantly arise and give forth a stench unendurable even on the bridge 40 or 50 feet above the surface."*

Marx records that the factory owners resisted all measures for maintaining cleanliness and health if they cut into profits.

SMART BLOKE, OLD MARX

BUT I DIDN'T HAVE ALL THE FACTS

ENGELS

MARX

Marx and Engels, living in the 19th century, saw and wrote about the environmental effects of capitalism. But they weren't too upset about the damage done to nature. In that age of boundless technological optimism *ecological principles were scarcely known — especially the basic idea that the Earth's resources are limited.

Marx seemed to view nature as a constant, static element – the unchanging background against which the class struggle would be fought out.

All human cultures encroach upon nature, altering their environments. But some act as if they owned it instead of being its trustees. Would Marx have revised his view of nature's role had he known that a century later environmental destruction would have reached a point where it threatened the very survival of humanity?

* The word 'œcology' was coined by the German Ernst Haeckel in 1866. It appeared in English as 'ecology' in 1893.

WELL, WHADDYOU THINK?

Some ecologists blame the Baconian creed . . .

WHAT'S THE BACONIAN CREED?

SCIENTIFIC KNOWLEDGE IS TECHNOLOGICAL POWER OVER NATURE

Francis Bacon, a 17th century British Lord Chancellor, provided the industrialists with a scientific alibi for their ruthless behaviour. Jailed for taking bribes, he eventually died of pneumonia while experimenting with frozen chicken.

WELL, AT LEAST THE EXPERIMENT WORKED

The Industrial Revolution stripped the Earth of its stored riches at an alarming rate, broke links with the soil (forcing Britain to import wheat) and pushed the farmer into the background. Populations exploded as technology 'mastered' the environment. Material wealth increased, at least in the West. But at what price?

"IF DIRECTED BY IGNORANCE, WEALTH IS A GREATER EVIL THAN POVERTY, BECAUSE IT CAN PUSH THINGS MORE STRONGLY IN THE WRONG DIRECTION."

PLATO

Industrialism spread from Britain to Europe and the United States.

BRINGING JOY AND PROGRESS

OR TURNING THE CLOCK BACK

Before the 17th century wealth per head in many parts of India, China, Africa and America was *higher* than in Europe.

WE HAD QUITE STABLE ECONOMIES

MIXED AGRICULTURE AND HANDICRAFTS

MEDICINE, MATHS, ASTRONOMY

IRON SMELTING, PRINTING, ADVANCED ENGINEERING

WE GENERALLY SUPPLIED OUR OWN NEEDS

European capitalism changed the whole picture.

FIRSTLY BY MILITARY PLUNDER AND SLAVERY...

AMERICA

EUROPE

SUGAR COTTON TOBACCO MOLASSES AND FAT PROFITS

TEXTILES AND GUNS

AFRICA

SLAVES

The Trade Triangle

...AND THEN BY ECONOMIC EXPLOITATION

Europe's industrialists turned the rest of the world into suppliers of food, raw materials and labour. Or markets for European manufactured goods.

OR BOTH

In 1660 the French traveller Bernier found Bengal (then part of India) to be richer even than Egypt. He wrote: *"It exports in abundance cottons and silks, rice, sugar and butter. It produces amply for its own consumption of wheat, vegetables, grains, fowls, ducks and geese. It has immense herds of pigs and flocks of sheep and goats. Fish of every kind it has in profusion."*

In 1757 the British soldier Clive reported Bengal's capital Murshidabad to be *"as extensive, populous and rich as the City of London"*.

Just 30 years of colonial rule later a British MP wrote of India: *"Many parts of these countries have been reduced to the appearance of a desert. The fields are no longer cultivated; extensive tracts are already overgrown with thickets; the husbandman is plundered; the manufacturer oppressed; famine has been repeatedly endured, and depopulation has ensued."*

Self-sufficiency was destroyed, leaving the colonies at the mercy of the world capitalist market. Mixed farming for subsistence was replaced by plantation farming of single 'cash crops' over vast areas – *monoculture!*

To the British ruling classes Ireland was just a source of cheap food — a wheat-growing colony. The Irish peasant's earnings were so small after rents and taxes that he had to grow potatoes to feed his family. Between 1700 and 1845 Ireland went from a grain-based to a potato-based agriculture. In 1845 the potato crop failed.

Starvation and hunger typhus killed two million Irish in four years, a quarter of the population. Two million more had to emigrate to the US and Canada. Many of them died en route in what came to be called the 'coffin ships'.

PROVIDENCE SENT THE POTATO BLIGHT
...

... BUT ENGLAND MADE THE FAMINE

Colonialist famine

In London the politicians were terribly concerned . . .
. . . about disrupting the grain market . . .

In 1847, when hundreds of
thousands were dying, food worth
17 million pounds was *exported*
from Ireland under the protection
of British troops.

The Irish were killed not just by
monoculture and famine but by
rent, profit and economic theory.

The Irish arrived in the US just in time to witness the annihilation of the greatest animal gathering in history – the buffalo herds of the Western Plains. The American Indian culture almost followed the buffalo into extinction.

THEY PROVIDED US WITH THE NECESSITIES OF LIFE

I KILLED 4,280 BUFFALO IN ONE YEAR

Tepees, food, clothing, bedding, fuel, bowstrings, glue, thread, cord, rope, saddle coverings, water vessels, boats and the means of purchasing all they wanted from the traders!

Systematic slaughter between 1850 and 1883 left only a few buffalo placed under protection as an embarrassed afterthought.

WE TREATED NATURE WITH HUMILITY AND RESPECT

WE VIEWED IT AS AN ENEMY TO BE OVERCOME

RESERVATION

Starting with George Washington in 1779 the US government had long used environmental destruction as a military weapon to subdue the Indians. At exactly the time he was planning to ruin the Iroquoi Nations' crops in northern New York honest George declared:

"The more I am acquainted with agricultural affairs the better I am pleased with them . . . I am led to reflect how much more delightful to an undebauched mind is the task of making improvements on the earth than all the vain glory which can be acquired from ravaging it"

The US Army consistently attacked the Indians' natural resources. Between 1860 and 1864 it wiped out the Navahos as a functioning society by destroying all their livestock, orchards and crops.

Eco-warfare was of course nothing new . . .

Imperialism

Towards the end of the 19th century the Golden Age of Industrialisation had used up so many raw materials and piled up so many goods that the need for new resources and markets became desperate. So while the US was grabbing colonies around the Americas the European capitalists carved up Africa among themselves.

In India the British had tried to impose their own ideas and practices, building giant canal, road and railway networks, and what one Englishman called 'the whole paraphernalia of a great civilised administration'. The result? Serious damage to the environment and severe nutritional problems for the rural masses, most of whom grew poorer.

Now it was the turn of Darkest Africa to be enlightened.

World War I was, among other things, a battle for resources between the empire-builders. At stake was the iron-rich Lorraine region (now part of France) as well as colonies and spheres of influence in Africa, eastern Asia and the Pacific. Over 15 million people were killed. In Europe, huge areas of farmland and forest were laid waste, especially in France and Belgium. Nature was also introduced to the delights of chemical warfare.

THE CHEMICAL INDUSTRY AND I JUST DON'T GET ON

Pressing ahead with the modernisation of 'backward' regions British engineers designed the first Aswan Dam on the River Nile in Egypt, promoting an epidemic of the parasitic disease *bilharzia*.

In the three years after the dam's completion in 1919 the disease increased five-fold. Today more than 50% of the population in five African nations have *bilharzia* or similar diseases. In some irrigated areas 100% of the local inhabitants are infected.

LOOK, I SAY, THE DAM THING TURNED DRYLANDS INTO FARMLANDS, DIDN'T IT ?

UPSTREAM, YES, BUT DOWNSTREAM IT MESSED UP FARMING AND FISHING

EVER HEARD OF AN ECOSYSTEM ?

BRITISH ENGINEER

FRESHWATER SNAIL (BILHARZIA CARRIER)

43

Meanwhile, the industrialists had come up with an impressive new way of poisoning the environment – mass motoring.

The petrol-powered automobile, symbol of the postwar economic boom, crashed into pedestrians, cyclists, horses, dogs, cats, trees, rivers, lamp-posts, shopfronts and, mostly, into other petrol-powered automobiles. The Great Crash, however, was not a traffic accident but a slump which depressed Western economies for years.

Life was particularly depressing for the American farmer. He was losing his soil. Erosion, caused mainly by monoculture (grain), artificial fertiliser, rash tree-cutting and ploughing up too much grassland, turned large regions of Oklahoma, Texas and Kansas into desert during the 1930s. It was called the Dust Bowl disaster. Credit banking played its part by forcing the farmers to over-exploit soil in order to meet interest payments.

Industrialisation speeded up human population growth dramatically. Birth rates rose and people lived longer. Technological progress generally made it easier to control famine and epidemic disease, two of the causes of high death-rates.

However, technology did not come to grips with the *third* cause — human aggression. Instead it increased man's destructive efficiency.

World War II cut the population by 50 million and wrecked cities, agriculture, forestry and ecosystems around the planet. One of Nazi Germany's justifications for waging war was 'lack of living space' . . .

To cap everything *homo sapiens* acquired the power that fires the sun and put it to use in the service of humanity . . .

Thus human civilisation in the mid-20th century reached a point where a single individual or small group could trigger immeasurable catastrophes affecting all life on Earth.

Environmental destruction

is any human activity that worsens the prospect for present or future generations to avail themselves of nature and survive within it. From that point of view the difference between agricultural societies and industrial societies is the difference between a light breeze and a storm. And comparing the first half of the 20th century with the last half is like comparing . . .

Post-war development was dedicated to the idea of unbridled technology and unlimited production and consumption. It fuelled the capitalist West and communist Eastern Europe alike. They disagreed on who should run things but shared the same production *goals* and *methods*, viewing nature as infinite and waste as no problem. So they caused the same kind of damage.

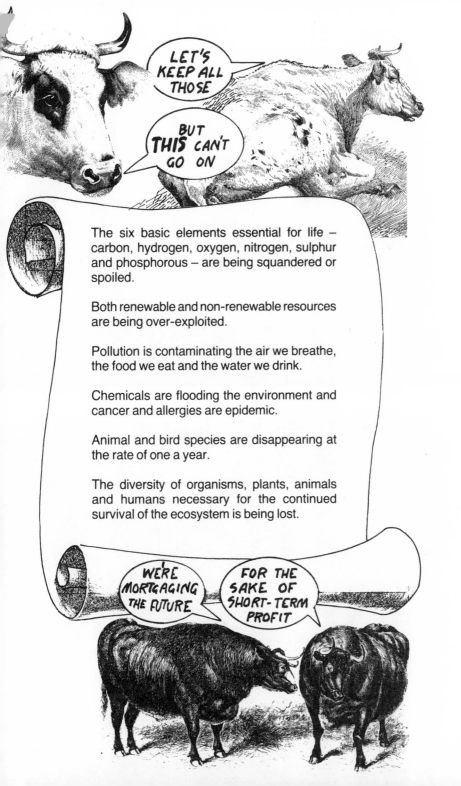

The six basic elements essential for life – carbon, hydrogen, oxygen, nitrogen, sulphur and phosphorous – are being squandered or spoiled.

Both renewable and non-renewable resources are being over-exploited.

Pollution is contaminating the air we breathe, the food we eat and the water we drink.

Chemicals are flooding the environment and cancer and allergies are epidemic.

Animal and bird species are disappearing at the rate of one a year.

The diversity of organisms, plants, animals and humans necessary for the continued survival of the ecosystem is being lost.

Protects
the car
against the
human race.

Mobil
super

because much of our time is spent working to buy time saving gadgets to do time consuming jobs

WHAT THE HELL IS GOING ON?

CARS DESERVE LOVING CARE, SAYS POPE

A car, according to the Pope, deserves the same loving care as the human soul.

During a visit to the Vatican's private garage yesterday, he told the Holy See's 40 drivers: "Your profession as chauffeurs should remind you continually that we are all on the road, heading at high speed towards eternity.

e do not have time for because much of our time is spent working to buy time saving gadgets to do time

Photosynthesis

Homo sapiens means Wise Man. It might have been wiser to have left the atom unsplit and let the sun provide the energy – as it had been doing extremely well for millions of years through *photosynthesis*.

The plants breathe in carbon dioxide, soak up the sun, draw water through their roots, breathe out oxygen and feed us. All life depends on greens.

Some scientists view this dependence as a problem and are trying to free humanity from 'green slavery' by the use of advanced technology (biotechnics).

Cycles

Green plants get their nutrition from the various 'cycles' of the biosphere, circulating energy and matter. Everything goes round and round, nothing is lost. Humans are the only species in natural history to produce things that can not be reabsorbed. The rest of nature completely converts 'waste' into resources.

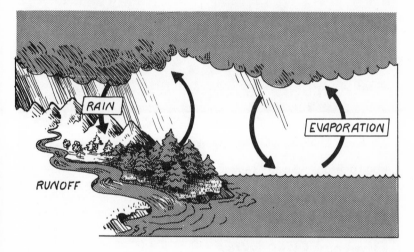

Less than 1% of the world's water is freshwater. It is scarce in most poor countries and is becoming scare as a result of industrialism in several rich countries.

Examples of water use:

1 kilo dry *wheat* – 1,500 litres
1 litre *milk* – 4,000 litres
1 kilo *meat* – 20-60,000 litres
1 *motorcar* – 400,000 litres

Carbon

All living things need carbon. In fact they're made from it. And so are a lot of dead things like coal, oil and diamonds.

Deforestation, pollution of the seas and heavy burning of fossil fuels are disturbing the flow of carbon through the cycle.

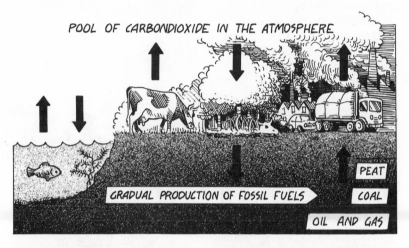

POOL OF CARBONDIOXIDE IN THE ATMOSPHERE

GRADUAL PRODUCTION OF FOSSIL FUELS

PEAT

COAL

OIL AND GAS

Carbon dioxide and water vapour in the atmosphere keep the Earth warm.

THIS IS THE GREENHOUSE EFFECT

If the heat were not trapped the global temperature would be about -24C (-10F) instead of about +16C (+60F).

Fossil-fuel combustion and other industrial activities are raising the carbon dioxide content of the atmosphere, which could raise the temperature. On the other hand the increasing presence of aerosols in the atmosphere, also due to industrial releases, could cool the Earth. Either way, weather conditions could be disastrously altered around the globe.

TRY GROWING WHEAT ON ICEBERGS!

Nitrogen   **+**   Phosphorous

becomes plant and animal protein, giving muscles, hair, bones, etc. The air is full of it. To be useful it must be 'fixed' in the form of ammonia. Fixing can occur naturally or be done artificially using natural gas – a process dominated by the US and the USSR.

comes from phosphate rock. It's an aid to root development and to energy storage in the seeds and fruit. It's also an essential element in DNA, the genetic 'messenger of life'. The US, USSR and Morocco produce 80% of all phosphate rock.

Fertiliser

has hooked most modern farmers on chemicals. It's an expensive habit both economically and ecologically, and hard to shake. Chemical fertiliser can increase yields in the short term but it promotes erosion by allowing the farmer to neglect soil maintenance. US agriculture is said to be using five times as much fertiliser today as in 1947 to produce the same amount of crops.

Apart from using up valuable non-renewable resources and turning plants into junkies, artificial fertiliser can have nasty side-effects, like disrupting neighbouring ecosystems.

The Healthy Food Chain

What happens to the clean-living, independent plant in a functioning ecosystem? The average blade of grass grows, using nutrients from the soil microbes, dies and rots, and is broken down by the microbes . . .

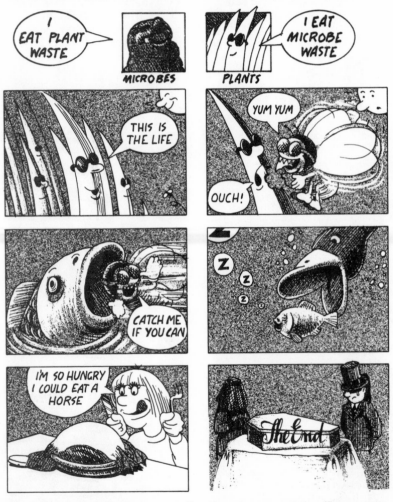

Cremating human bodies, or sealing them in graveyard coffins, means that the fertility which the blade of grass 'borrowed' from the soil is lost. The chain is broken.

Web, niche & pyramid

SOUNDS LIKE A LAW FIRM

All food chains start with plants. Usually there are only two or three links and almost never more than four, including the *herbivore* (plant-eater) and *carnivore* (flesh-eater).

There are millions of different chains. The sum total of chains in any community is called the *food web*.

Complicated? This is only *part* of a food web

Well before the ecologists arrived on the scene Darwin had described nature as 'a web of complex relations'. But he saw life as a competitive struggle for existence won by the strongest of the species. His theory of 'natural selection' delighted the aggressive Victorian capitalists. But a century later it would give way to a view of nature stressing interaction and cooperation, cycles and energy transfers.

MY IDEAS EVOLVED IN INDUSTRIA CLIMATE

Darwin showed that every species had its 'place' in nature. This came to be termed the *ecological niche*. It may be filled by different species in different areas. Grass-eaters may be kangaroos in Australia and cattle on the Argentine pampas.

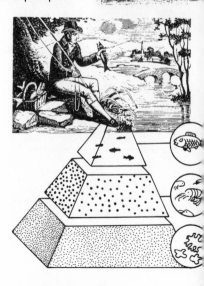

In general the higher up the food chain you go the bigger and fewer the species.

This is the *pyramid* concept. We humans sit at the top of many food pyramids.

The Unhealthy Food Chain

SPIDER MITE

Chemical pesticides like DDT do a more thorough job on the predators than on the pests! The pests are more numerous so they adapt. The predators, their *natural* enemies, are vulnerable because the fartherup the food chain the DDT travels the more it is concentrated.

Pesticides by removing the biological checks can even create new pests. Once-harmless insects breed out of control when the next ones up in the pecking order are removed.

Like artificial fertiliser, pesticides lead farmers to greater and greater chemical dependency, upset ecosystems and spread through food chains, joining many other varieties of poisonous waste in human bodies. Their interaction is largely unknown.

DDT is banned in most industrialised countries but its *overall* use is still increasing and the effects are spread globally by wind and water.

59

Stable

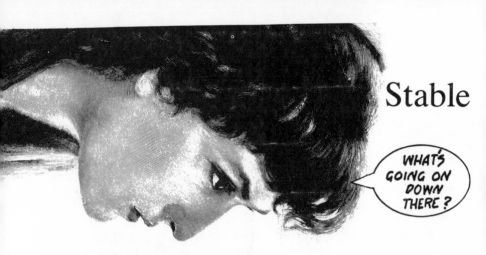

WHAT'S GOING ON DOWN THERE?

A gram of fertile soil contains about 100 million living bacteria. A square metre of farmland can be inhabited by 55 million worms and 50,000 small insects and mites. The total mass of microbe life on the planet has been estimated at 25 times the total mass of all animal life.

Agribusiness, modern capitalist farming, isn't interested in these little creatures. For quick profit it 'mines' or 'quarries' the soil, drenching it in lethal and persistent poisons and ignoring the long-term effects.

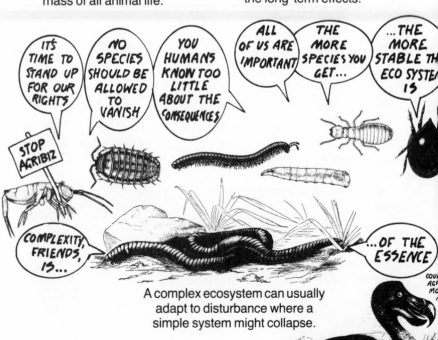

IT'S TIME TO STAND UP FOR OUR RIGHTS

NO SPECIES SHOULD BE ALLOWED TO VANISH

YOU HUMANS KNOW TOO LITTLE ABOUT THE CONSEQUENCES

ALL OF US ARE IMPORTANT

THE MORE SPECIES YOU GET...

...THE MORE STABLE TH ECO SYSTE IS

STOP AGRIBIZ

COMPLEXITY, FRIENDS, IS...

...OF THE ESSENCE

A complex ecosystem can usually adapt to disturbance where a simple system might collapse.

& unstable

Ever since farming began humanity has been an enemy of complexity in nature and therefore a *destabilising* force. Only recently have we begun to realise that losing plant and animal species isn't a trivial matter to be mourned only by nature-lovers but a dangerous and irreversible tinkering with the natural systems on which we depend.

Agribiz is the big culprit. Driven by commercial interest it disregards flavour, food value, resistance to disease, adaptability . . . in short, plant *diversity*. To control the market it's buying up the seed trade and reducing the line to a few patentable, single-season, expensive hybrids dependent on the fertiliser and pesticide which it also sells. To the multinationals biological simplicity makes economic sense. They're filling the world's grainfields with armies of cloned, drugged, sterile zombies requiring constant vigilance and inputs of energy to stave off collapse.

ALL MAJOR food crops grown in the United States originated outside the country. For Americans there is really no such thing as a home-grown meal. Wheat, spinach and apples derive from Asia, soybeans from China, corn and tomatoes from Central America, potatoes from the Andes, and sorghum from Africa.

This means that the United States is almost entirely dependent on genetic supplies for its agriculture from outside the country, and especially from the tropics. Without constant infusions of fresh germplasm, the productivity of modern crops cannot be maintained, let alone expanded. It is the skills of plant geneticists, rather than large amounts of artificial additives such as pesticides and fertilisers, that have led to one record after another in crop yields in the United States.

Since the United States is so dependent on exotic genetic resources, its agricultural situation is, according to the Department of Agriculture, "serious, potentially dangerous to the welfare of the nation, and growing worse." Not surprisingly, then the past few years have seen American plant collectors searching for germplasm in many gene-rich localities abroad. They have been looking for virus-resistant barley and super-productive germplasm for peas in Ethiopia, for more nutritious strains of potatoes in Peru, for disease-resistant varieties of wheat in Turkey and Afghanistan, and for wild and primitive strains of corn in Central America.

The Great Pea Grab

In short, the United States faces a situation of "genetic wipe-out." At the same time, certain tropical countries are beginning to realise that their gene reservoirs represent scarce resources that are becoming increasingly crucial to the great grain-growing belts of the world, notably in the zone extending across North America.

Among US Government agencies to turn an eye to the problem is the Central Intelligence Agency. The agency believes it exercises partial responsibility for supplies of raw materials that are critical to the US economy. Hence the CIA's recent interest in gene reservoirs overseas that could become increasingly important to US agriculture; and the agency is assessing the political proclivities of the countries in question, to determine whether they will remain "suitably disposed" to the United States.

Who knows, the day may arrive when US Marines are launched on foreign raids, not to rescue a group of hostages, but to seize a few wild specimens of a crop plant growing in some foreign field.

"Guardian, November 6, 1980"

A Day in the Life of the Eighties

A disturbing tale of a modern nuclear family in contemporary society somewhere in the West

At home

Doris is a pill-popper. She takes them to calm down, to perk up and to go to sleep.

Tranquillisers against stress have created a serious drug addiction problem in the Western world. Valium, the bestseller in a range of 700 depressants, is prescribed 50 million times a year in the US and 20 million times in Europe. Women use twice as much as men. It can be dangerously toxic and produce classic withdrawal symptoms. It earns nearly 1,000 million dollars a year for its makers, Hoffman-LaRoche.

Doris also uses cosmetics although they give her a skin rash. She has seen enough ads to know how the 'ideal woman' is supposed to look. The ad-man 'steals her love of herself as she is and offers it back to her for the price of the product' (John Berger).

The Lee family has little time to make fresh food. It has become dependent on expensive but nutritionally poor processed foods, marketed by an industry that is concerned not with health but with profit. The big retailing companies also control a major part of food production.

THOSE BATTERY EGGS COST SIX TIMES MORE ENERGY TO PRODUCE THAN THEY GIVE IN FOOD VALUE

Computers are taking over in many walks of life. They have their advantages but they make it easier for authorities and commercial interests to keep tabs on the private citizen and to centralise power. Interpersonal contact is reduced. It becomes harder to 'wipe the slate clean' and start afresh.

BUT WE DON'T EVEN HAVE GAS

GAS BILL
PAY UP OR ELSE
£ 1,000,000

Off to work

The Lees travel a lot. They sleep in one place, work or attend school in another, shop in a third, seek entertainment in a fourth, pursue sports or creative activities in a fifth and 'consume' nature in a sixth.

CAN'T WAIT TO GET A PEDAL CAR

AHH.., FREEDOM

GREG 1

Motor exhaust fumes contain about 1,000 toxic elements and cause 60-90% of all air pollution in industrialised countries. Carbon monoxide is especially dangerous for weak hearts as it reduces oxygen intake, hydro-carbon causes fatigue and possibly cancer, lead can damage children's brains. Motor vehicles also fill our lungs with dust particles from road surfaces and asbestos from brake drums.

OH F....

The automobile is following Greg from the cradle to the grave. He was born in the back seat of a taxi and will die in the front seat of his car with a broken spine and a smashed chassis. Doris goes to work by bus. Julie cycles to school.

HOPE THERE'S ROOM

WISH THERE WERE BICYCLE LANES

In Europe 16 firms are producing seven million cars of 300 different makes every year. Mass motoring drains oil and mineral resources, fouls the air, makes a lot of noise and eats up both land for roads and investment funds badly needed for public transport. The average carrying rate is 1.3 persons per car so it takes 300 cars to transport 400 people – a queue 5 kilometres long.

A train 150 metres long can perform the same task at a fraction of the cost to the economy and the environment.

On the job

Doris Lee works on an assembly line. The job is monotonous, requiring little thought or skill, but the fast pace means she can never relax. Doris views the machinery as an enemy. As for the product, she has no idea how it's planned or marketed. She'd like to change her job but doesn't dare because of the high unemployment rate. At the end of the day she rarely has enough energy left to engage in union activity.

Greg Lee works in a factory sales department. His office is clean and quiet. He has never handled a machine and has no idea how the product is put together. Out of touch with the shopfloor, he views the labour force in purely economic terms and agrees with his boss that the unions are troublemakers. Management wants to replace workers with industrial robots and is sending a man to check fully-automated Japanese factories run by a handful of electro-engineers.

In hospital

Arthur Lee is in hospital for heart trouble. The place is modern, large, often crowded and short-staffed. Arthur's not sure how ill he is or what treatment he's receiving. No-one has much time for him. He feels small and lonely.

The industrialised countries are getting more and more doctors, more and more hospitals – and more and more sick people. Costs and medicine consumption are going up but there's no corresponding improvement in public health and life expectancy. Over 75% of deaths are from cancer, heart and respiratory diseases and accidents. These result from oppressive environments and lifestyles, and medical science can do little about them.

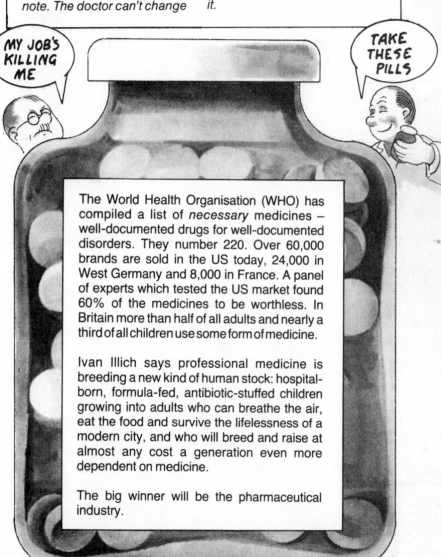

Arthur long ago lost the right to declare himself sick. Only his doctor can do that, with a sick note. The doctor can't change Arthur's social and economic situation but he can give him drugs to stop him worrying about it.

MY JOB'S KILLING ME

TAKE THESE PILLS

The World Health Organisation (WHO) has compiled a list of *necessary* medicines – well-documented drugs for well-documented disorders. They number 220. Over 60,000 brands are sold in the US today, 24,000 in West Germany and 8,000 in France. A panel of experts which tested the US market found 60% of the medicines to be worthless. In Britain more than half of all adults and nearly a third of all children use some form of medicine.

Ivan Illich says professional medicine is breeding a new kind of human stock: hospital-born, formula-fed, antibiotic-stuffed children growing into adults who can breathe the air, eat the food and survive the lifelessness of a modern city, and who will breed and raise at almost any cost a generation even more dependent on medicine.

The big winner will be the pharmaceutical industry.

Out to lunch

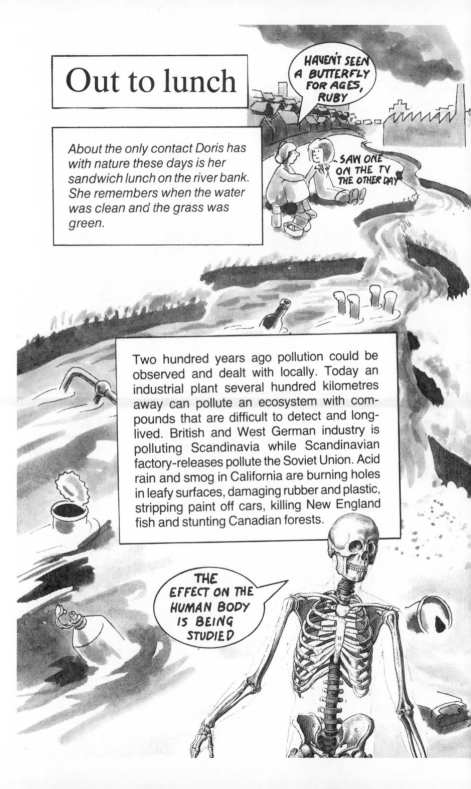

About the only contact Doris has with nature these days is her sandwich lunch on the river bank. She remembers when the water was clean and the grass was green.

HAVEN'T SEEN A BUTTERFLY FOR AGES, RUBY

SAW ONE ON THE TV THE OTHER DAY

Two hundred years ago pollution could be observed and dealt with locally. Today an industrial plant several hundred kilometres away can pollute an ecosystem with compounds that are difficult to detect and long-lived. British and West German industry is polluting Scandinavia while Scandinavian factory-releases pollute the Soviet Union. Acid rain and smog in California are burning holes in leafy surfaces, damaging rubber and plastic, stripping paint off cars, killing New England fish and stunting Canadian forests.

THE EFFECT ON THE HUMAN BODY IS BEING STUDIED

Meanwhile Greg is at the hamburger bar polluting himself and people around him.

I'M REALLY STUFFED

Apart from nicotine and tar, cigarette smoke contains some 2,000 chemical compounds.

A New Yorker walking the streets for a whole day breathes in the toxic equivalent of two packets of cigarettes.

Medical evidence shows that the combination of a high-fat diet, tobacco smoking and stress strongly suggests a heart attack after 40, especially in overweight people. Modern food is designed to be over-eaten. The industry is pushing food with little bulk and a high energy content, such as sweets, Coca-Cola and ice cream. A Norwegian ecologist says we spend 10 times as much on repairing the damage caused by over-eating as we spend on trying to eliminate the protein shortage in the Third World.

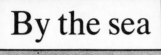

By the sea

Julie Lee is on a school outing.

LOVELY WEATHER!

Industrialism and deforestation are disrupting the carbon cycle to such an extent that scientists are predicting the warmest temperatures since before the last Ice Age by the middle of the next century. A CIA 'future scenario' says this could mean wrecked crops in the main food belts, famine, economic instability, civil unrest and even war. In the long term it could melt polar icecaps and raise sea-levels throughout the world.

In 1970 the explorer Thor Heyerdahl, crossing the Atlantic in a papyrus boat, noted oil clots on 43 of the journey's 57 days. Oil often ends up on ocean shores, where most marine life passes one stage of its life cycle.

In the country

Julie Lee's grandparents are buried near the small farm where they worked most of their lives and raised Doris. It has been sold for road and property development.

Precious agricultural land is being lost at twice the rate that new land is being broken. An area bigger than Britain is disappearing every year. Soil is being exhausted and eroded or it is vanishing beneath motorways, urban spread, airports and industrial development. Or it's becoming wasteland. If this goes on, by the end of the century the world may have to support 1½ times the present population on only ¾ of its present cultivated area.

AND I'M BEING DISPLACED TOO

YESTERDAY'S FARMWORKER IS TODAY'S CANNER, TRACTOR MECHANIC OR FAST FOOD DELIVERY MAN

AGRI BIZ

Down on the big farm next door, biocides (life-killers) are accumulating in the food chain . . . just like in Vietnam.

For over 30 years farmworkers, forestry workers and the public have been exposed to sprayings of the 'weedkiller' 245-T. It contains dioxin, one of the most poisonous substances known. The Americans used 245-T under the name of Agent Orange to defoliate Vietnam. They sprayed 10.7 million gallons, highly concentrated with dioxin, over 3 million acres, which led to widespread miscarriages, deformities and liver cancer, mostly among the Vietnamese but also among US servicemen and their children. Vietnamese are still at risk today, more than a decade after the spraying ended.

YOU CAN'T PROVE A THING

245-T is now banned in Sweden, Holland and Italy. In the US and Britain the agro-chemical industry strongly opposed union efforts to have it outlawed.

DOW

At the shops

Doris Lee doesn't know the staff at the giant supermarket which has replaced her local shops. To them she is just another face in the crowd. She can afford more in her trolley nowadays but she has a feeling she is not getting more for her money.

Shoddy goods squander energy and raw materials while keeping profits up. Unnecessary packaging, especially throwaway containers, add to the problem – and the profits. The average American throws away over two kilos of household waste a day, the average Briton almost a kilo. Most of it could be recycled.

Doris, like most Westerners, spends a third of her income on food. In other words a third of her working life is concerned with getting food – exactly like the hunters and gatherers of early times!

The broiler chicken is the most industrialised of all animal foods. It's a little meat machine, bred to live just six months in a giant factory, sitting in a cage, scarcely moving, almost always eating, under constant medication, pumped with growth hormones and, if it survives the stress, finally slaughtered by an assembly line.

WHAT A LIFE!

FACTORY PIGS AREN'T MUCH BETTER OFF

IF YOU REALLY WANT A HORROR STORY TRY US

The TV commercials are also teaching comparison. Julie is being urged to keep up, to strive for the better life of glamour and luxury.

BATHE IN THE CHAMPAGNE SURF

Capitalism and consumerism are always raising the stakes. They deal in frustration by constantly heightening expectations. As soon as something is available to everyone it is 'no longer attractive'. If you had a radio yesterday you must have a colour TV today and a home-video tomorrow. New 'demands' are created by producing and promoting new articles and activities that in fact are accessible only to an élite group of extravagant consumers. Illich calls this process 'modernising poverty'.

PAUL HARRISON SAYS :- relative poverty can be almost as destructive as absolute poverty because it can preoccupy or even obsess your thoughts and divert you from the enjoyment of your life . . .

AND HE'S RIGHT.

The same evening

Doris is daydreaming. She remembers when she and Arthur had the time and energy to cycle into the country, pick berries and lie among the wildflowers. In their old home he enjoyed doing carpentry in the back yard. Since moving to the housing estate the only things he has made with his hands have been matchstick cathedrals.

HE MOSTLY JUST BOOZES THESE DAYS

THE WHOLE NEIGHBOURHOOD'S BLACKED OUT

OI, SOMEONE FIX THE FUSE

SECOND TIME THIS MONTH

THE DINNER WON'T COOK! AND THE FROZEN FOOD WILL ROT!

I'M OFF FOR A DRINK

NO TV. BUT WHO CARES?

Central energy systems built on a few large power stations are far more vulnerable than small local systems. A mixture of small systems is also more adaptable to technological and social change. As in the ecosystem variety means resilience.

Nuclear power is complex and dangerous. It provides baseload electricity for the grid. Most people in the industrialised countries are plugged into grid electricity, like it or not. The individual consumer has no influence on prices. You either pay up or get cut off, even if the choice is between eating and keeping warm.

The drive for big systems has meant that two-thirds of world energy now comes from irreplaceable assets: coal, oil, natural gas, uranium and lignite. Humanity today consumes more coal in a single day than was generated in a hundred centuries or so during the process of carbonisation.

That night

Greg

dreams of a white super-race produced by genetic engineering. So as not to pollute the gene pool non-whites have been exterminated along with the mentally ill, the physically handicapped and the homosexuals. Women are either in bed or in the kitchen.

Arthur

dreams he has stopped drinking and shouting at his family. Since going on to a short working week he has taken up carpentry again at the neighbourhood workshop. He earns quite a lot doing odd jobs and feels useful and creative.

Julie

dreams she's learning how to work with leather and stone at a school where no one's forced to attend lessons, academic certificates don't exist and afternoons are spent outdoors. The Labour Exchange has been turned into a Free Activity Centre.

Doris

dreams she's a vegetable gardener far from noise, stress and pollution. Her work is varied and meaningful. She feels healthy, playing an active role in a community where everyone knows everyone else. She has stopped taking pills.

The Lees are victims of an economic theory that makes no sense in human or ecological terms. It ruins their physical environment and their mental well-being.

Modern humanity can now reach all parts of the biosphere, from the deepest oceans to the farthest reaches of the sky, and communicate almost instantly. But its failure to control technology and treat the land sensibly means that the body fat of every person on the planet now contains DDT and that agriculture, the 'basic interface between human societies and their environment', is rapidly *destroying* soil while millions starve to death.

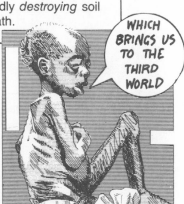

WHICH BRINGS US TO THE THIRD WORLD

Water & Fuel

Life in the Third World is mainly a struggle for survival.

In parts of Africa women today have to walk 15 or 20 kilometres to fetch water, leaving at dusk and returning at dawn. In Africa and South and East Asia only 1/5 of the rural population has reasonable access to a safe water supply.

Almost every tubewell wound up as the property of one man – the rich landowner who could bribe the local authorities. He can sell 'his' water at his own price, which is often too high for the other village farmers.

The World Bank lent Bangladesh funds for 3,000 tubewells. Each was supposed to provide irrigation for 25-50 farmers.

So the tubewell is being under-used at the same time as the large landowner is better placed to buy out his poor neighbours when hard times fall.

Over 85% of wood cut in the Third World is used for fuel. At the present rate 40% of the remaining forest will be gone by 2000.

Fuel is so scarce in some African areas that crop residues and stubble are now being burned although they are desperately needed as humus (plant nutrients) to bind the soil.

Indian farmland is likewise losing its fertility because the firewood shortage is forcing peasants to burn cow dung, which now accounts for ¾ of domestic fuel consumption!

On Java, forested slopes have been reduced to crumbling cliffs as land hunger pushes peasants higher and higher up mountainsides.

Erosion

Desert

Large areas of the world's desert ecosystems are being degraded by overgrazing, bad farming and deforestation.

The deserts are advancing, particularly in India and the Sahel, the vast dryland region of Africa along the southern Sahara.

But the deserts are also retreating, *eg* in Algeria, Israel and China where governments are restoring farmland and orchards.

Desert spread is not inevitable. It depends on what action is taken by humans. Erosion in the Third World occurs largely because fertile land is monopolised by a few, forcing the majority of farmers to over-use vulnerable soil.

Until colonialism came, pastoral nomads herding animals around the Sahel fully utilised the semi-arid desert's few resources.

They moved according to the cycles of nature, kept mixed herds to exploit the various ecological niches, swapped meat and dairy products for the farmers' grain and manured their lands.

The French changed all that. Taxes forced the nomads to deal in money and rely on the 'market'. Their pastures were turned over to peanut and cotton production for export, their movements were restricted and the demand for beef made them give up mixed herds for cattle.

To compensate they have built up herds, with the aid of modern medicine, beyond the carrying capacity of the land left to them.

Tropical rain forest is one of the planet's great biological resources. It has developed an enormously efficient ecosystem over 50 million years. But the system is fragile because the topsoil is shallow and the lush growth is largely water, disguising a low level of fertility. It's the dense tree cover that keeps the system going. Without it the soil is easily washed away.

Plant and animal life in tropical rain forests is simply not equipped to deal with sudden and drastic large-scale change. It's no match for legions of giant bulldozers, chainsaws, fire-teams and biocides – the tools being used to destroy the rain forests at a rate of more than 100,000 acres a day.

To strip tropical rain forest is to wipe out for ever the end-product of millenia of evolution (the surviving ancestral species from which most of today's 10 million species have descended), to prevent the study of thousands of undescribed plants and animals, to ruin beauty and to endanger the survival of the remaining 'primitive' cultural groups living there.

Jungle

The Amazon rain forest is a world lung. It is believed to provide ¼ of all our oxygen. Today this supply is dwindling because of Brazil's military government. It is selling off the Amazon to private firms for exploration, mining, timber and ranching. Multi-nationals like Nestlé, Goodyear, Volkswagen and Mitsubishi are 'making a killing'.

IF THE JUNGLES GO, THE WORLD SUFFOCATES

BRAZIL'S RICH, BUT WE'RE POOR

Who has benefited from Brazil's 'economic boom'? In the 1950s half the population had jobs. Today only a third can find work. The *minifundios* (minimal smallholdings) are being swallowed up by the *latifundios* (big estates), which under-use the land and do not bother to modernise agriculture because there is abundant cheap labour. Surveys show that by nutritional standards the people of 'booming' Brazil are worse off than the people of 'stagnating' Sri Lanka or Burma.

The Green Revolution

In many Third World areas the Green Revolution is replacing mixed crop strains with uniform, short-stemmed hybrids of rice, wheat and maize specially bred to respond to chemical fertiliser, herbicides, pesticides and careful irrigation. They are hypersensitive, totally reliant on their magic ingredients.

Food production is increasing. *But so is starvation*! The Green Revolution and the mechanisation of agriculture accompanying it have enriched the already well-off while creating unemployment and pushing the small farmer and the landless further below the poverty line.

Their ability to buy food is reduced. Capacity grows but 'demand' does not. Mountains of grain rot in countries where people go hungry.

Wealthy farmers and landlords reap the benefits of modern technology while the rural masses are denied access to land and forced into wage labour – but there's less and less work because of mechanisation. Peasant resistance is violently repressed by the big landowners and their allies, the police and magistrates.

Biologically, the Green Revolution is a poor bet because of the risks of plant disease, pests, erosion and the heavy drain on fuel and fertiliser resources. In the long run it can lead to ecological collapse and far greater human misery.

Cash Crops

Impoverishment of the soil is no natural disaster. It is mainly a result of Western demand for meat and luxury 'colonial goods'.

Cash-cropping monoculture is steadily replacing traditional techniques that protected the soil. Worldwide, almost 640,000 sq. km. are given over to cash crops of little or no nutritional value. Providing what?

Sugar for the sweet Western tooth
Tea & coffee for Western drinkers
Tobacco for Western smokers
Cotton for Western jeans
Cut flowers for Western vases
Peanuts for Western parties
Feed for Western livestock

Ecologically damaging Western practices are not only to be found in agriculture. Almost all the non-communist states of the Third World are being 'Westernised'. Their rulers were often educated in the West or racially humiliated under colonialism. Many of them now seem intent on 'out-Westernising' the West!

These national élites join forces with the multinational corporations to introduce the West's big-scale technology, standardised mass culture, middle-class lifestyles and values into economies which can afford none of them and traditional societies which cannot survive alongside them. The 'Western way' tends to reduce humanity's cultural diversity.

Malnutrition

The Green Revolution hybrids displace pulses and other protein-rich crops, thereby adding to the malnutrition that's undermining human capacity in the Third World. Protein deficiency impairs brain development in infants and the damage cannot be undone later.

The WHO says that 100 million of the world's 300 million children under five are suffering from protein energy malnutrition. Under-nourished children have smaller heads than normal. Their brains don't fill their skulls properly. Those who survive infancy grow up chronically malnourished and slip easily into a vicious circle of deprivation . . .

The multinationals are flooding the Third World with products that are useless or directly harmful or both. With one hand they steal the protein from the poor and serve it up as steak, bacon, eggs and milk for Western tables. With the other they pump into the Third World things like Ritz crackers, chewing gum, ITT's Hostess Twinkies cupcakes, white bread, Coke, Fanta, Pepsi, Frosted Flakes, as well as high-tar cigarettes and drugs banned in the West.

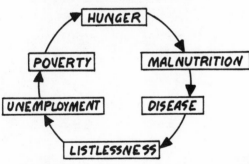

In the Third World 75% of premature deaths are caused by parasitic or infectious disease. In most cases malnutrition has contributed.

Breastmilk is an invaluable source of nutrition. Firms like Nestlé and Cow & Gate have helped persuade Third World mothers to give it up in favour of their formula babyfoods. As a result WHO studies show malnutrition setting in at eight months instead of 18 months in several countries.

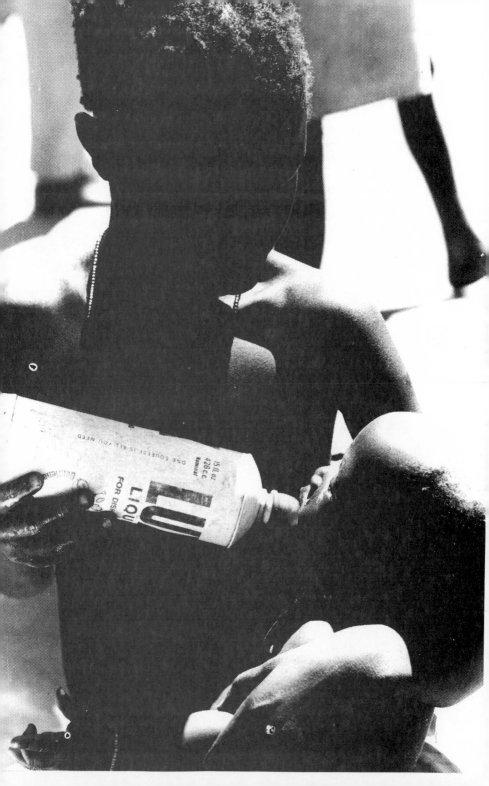

Population

The present human population is over four billion. It took 100,000 years to reach that figure. It looks like taking 40-50 years to add another four billion.

I'M THE ONLY ANIMAL WHO CAN KEEP UP

HOW MUCH CAN I TAKE?

No-one is sure of the Earth's maximum 'carrying-capacity'. One UN report suggests 36 billion. The US National Academy of Sciences estimates 30 billion. Others put the figure lower.

For the starving villagers of the Third World, where population growth is fastest, the question holds no interest. Children are usually the only resource they can rely on. The rest is owned by the rich.

Birth rates generally do not fall until levels of living improve — or until poverty is so great that new children are more of a burden than an asset.

Birth control is necessary, not least to liberate the countless women for whom unsafe abortions are the only alternative to a life of endless pregnancies. And too many people in one place can overtax local eco-systems.

But 'over-population' is essentially too many people with too little access to *the means of production and consumption*. This is a political problem. To adopt family planning policies that simply aim 'to stop the poor from breeding' is to treat the unequal distribution of wealth and power as if it were a biological problem rather than the direct result of the capitalist system.

It is small wonder that in the absence of overall development programmes poor families view birth-control devices with suspicion.

THANKS BUT WE'D RATHER HAVE OUR LAND BACK

Two roads

India

"We're opposed to radical political change so we use repression and the new technology to try and enforce population control"

China

"Socialists seek to limit the birthrate by raising the standard of health and education, involving people in ownership and guaranteeing them security in old age"

LOOK AFTER THE PEOPLE AND LET THE POPULATION LOOK AFTER ITSELF

Education of girls is a key to lower birthrates. Parents no longer feel the need for such large families when daughters can support them as well as sons, while educated women have more say in when they marry, when they have children and how many.

Nature has built a 'genetic brake' into the reproductive systems of many animal species.

Could this also be the case for human beings? There's evidence that women everywhere seem to *want* fewer children these days, even if circumstances do not allow them to. As for the men, some of them seem intent on depopulating the world once and for all . . .

While the world population is still growing the *rate of increase* is slowing down. But many poor countries will double their numbers within a generation and regional 'overcrowding' will be a problem for at least another century.

The longer it takes to introduce ecologically sound farming practices and radical land reforms the more terrifying is the prospect for the world's poor — and for world peace.

Resources

LET'S GET ONE THING STRAIGHT

There is no world shortage of food.

BUT I THOUGHT..

There is enough food in the world today to feed everyone. The problem is that it's not being shared out fairly.

DO YOU MEAN...?

And that applies to most resources. It's not population pressure that's gobbling them up but wasteful production and consumption in the industrialised world.

I REALLY MUST PROTEST!

The West takes 2/3 of world fossil fuel imports, 3/4 of metal ores, and 4/5 of non-ferrous metals. The average American uses 13 times as much energy as a Latin American, 20 times as much as an Asian and 30 times as much as an African.

BLOODY SCANDAL!

Food. The world grain trade is controlled by five private corporations: Continental Grain and Cargill (US), Bunge (US-Brazil), Louis Dreyfus (France) and André (Switzerland).

Energy. Seven private oil companies control the petroleum industry: Exxon, Mobil, Gulf, Shell, Texaco, Standard and BP.

Metals. Six aluminium producers control bauxite production: Alcoa, Alcan, Reynolds, Kaiser, Anaconda and Revere. INCO (Canada) and Le Nickel (France) dominate the nickel industry. The oil companies are assuming control of the copper trade.

Sea. Six mining consortia have been formed to exploit the ocean bed's mineral resources (including manganese, nickel, cobalt, copper, aluminium, iron).

Land. Worldwide 30% of landowners own 80% of the land. The large landowners are the least productive.

Scarcity

'If we seek to devise a way of life that can continue, in safety, into the remote future, then we would do well to base that way of life on the use of resources that will remain easily obtainable and plentiful for as long as the Earth continues to exist. Where we are dependent on resources that can be exhausted it would be wise to free ourselves from such dependence.'

— from The Little Green Book

Resource estimates are notoriously unreliable. They keep changing as new deposits are located. But the general trend is that resources are becoming harder and harder to get at. The oilmen and miners are having to dig deeper or develop new technology, using ever more energy, all of which are expensive.

So even if a resource doesn't vanish completely it's increasingly concentrated in the hands of the rich and powerful, until it's no longer profitable to recover.

In such a 'scarcity economy' life and death can be determined by which class you belong to.

SCARCITY JUST MEANS A RESOURCE CAN'T BE RECOVERED SO PROFITABLY

The flow of the world's resources is dictated by the rich, often through the multinationals, who it is estimated will control 80% of *all production* in the capitalist world by 1985. These 'monopoly capitalists', now a law unto themselves, have built their position on cheap energy and raw materials. As they become scarce and the Third World struggles to hold on to its own assets today's 'peaceful' methods of exploitation will no longer do the trick.

To survive, industrial capitalism will have to embark on new and even more destructive 'crusades' in the southern biosphere.

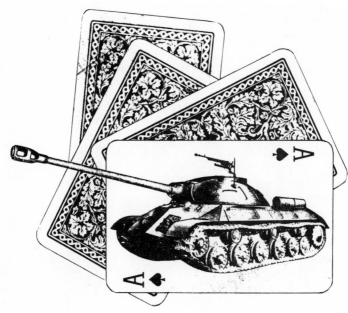

Whose needs?

A lot of people around the planet aren't feeling too well. Their needs aren't being met. What *do* they need?

THINGS ARE LOOKING A BIT GRIM

Protected Species

TO BE LOVED AND TOUCHED

FED CLOTHED AND HOUSED

HEALTH AND EDUCATION

COMPANIONSHIP

ENVIRONMENT

RIGHTS AND FREEDOM

SURVIVAL JUSTICE AND SELF-DEFINED WORK

What does Illich mean by self-defined work?

"People need not only to obtain things, they need above all the freedom to make things among which they can live, or give shape to them according to their own tastes, and to put them to use in caring about others"
— from Tools for Conviviality

Hi, I'm Ivan Illich

110

Economists don't concern themselves with people's inner feelings, hopes and dreams.

WHAT'S RIGHT FOR THE ECONOMY IS RIGHT FOR HUMANITY

Forced to adapt to the needs of an oppressive economic system, people easily lose touch with what's good for them and punish not only themselves and their fellow-beings but also the animals and plants that surround them.

THE "BRAINS"

'Modern capitalism needs men who cooperate smoothly and in large numbers; who want to consume more and more; and whose tastes are standardised and can be easily influenced and anticipated. It needs men who feel free and independent, not subject to any authority or principle or conscience –yet willing to be commanded, to do what is expected of them, to fit into the social machine without friction; who can be guided without force, led without leaders, prompted without aim, except the one to make good, to be on the move, to function, to go ahead.

What is the outcome? Modern man is alienated from himself, from his fellow men, and from nature'

– Erich Fromm, The Art of Loving

NO WONDER MAN OPPRESSES WOMAN!

111

Capitalism

The capitalist market meets people's needs only when it's profitable to do so. It is only interested in who can buy what.

The law of the market is that 'purchasing power' rules. Only those who have it can demand to be supplied while the rest can whistle in the dark.

The market economy allows capitalism to go on producing only what is profitable for capitalism, whatever the price to the environment and without regard for people's real needs.

Under pressure, capitalism becomes a bit more 'eco-conscious' and instals filters, scrubbers, purifying plant, etc. These aren't to be coughed at (even if they're often paid for by the public authorities out of taxpayers' money) but repairing damage to the environment involves delayed action, which can be perilous. Why not organise things properly from the start instead of spending more and more to keep the whole show together?

Today's capitalist crisis is partly an eco-crisis. Industry is running out of elbow-room. Not only is it having to dig deeper, build higher and pay more for land and energy but it is also having to recirculate air and water. What used to be free is now expensive. It has to be *reproduced*.

By misusing resources that in principle are renewable – air and water, farmland and forest – capitalism has run up against *physical limits*. To ensure continued growth it tries to raise prices . . .

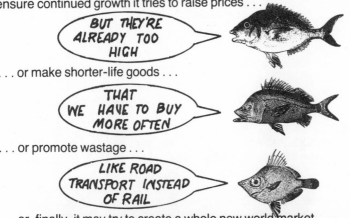

. . . or make shorter-life goods . . .

. . . or promote wastage . . .

. . . or, finally, it may try to create a whole new world market . . .

Growth & misgrowth

Today, economic growth under capitalism means the growth of pollution, consumerism, alienation, inequality, ill-health and the risk of war.

We've reached a point where 'more' often means 'worse' and people are finding that 'less' can be the key to a better living standard. Isn't it better to create as *few* needs as possible and satisfy them with the *smallest* possible consumption of raw materials, energy and work so as to cause the *least* possible damage?

The longer capitalism is allowed to rule the economy the greater is the danger of a total ecological collapse. The sooner production-for-profit is replaced by production-for-needs the better are the chances of human survival and happiness.

AND THAT GOES FOR THE REST OF US TOO!

CHOOSE SOCIALISM OR BARBARISM!

In a planned economy it becomes possible to achieve a relationship between human society and nature that's *co-existing* rather than *conflicting*. But from an ecological point of view socialism is no alternative to capitalism as long as it shares the same emphasis on industrial development and the same production goals and methods.

CAPITALISM IS ANTI-ECOLOGY. BUT SOCIALISM IS NOT NECESSARILY PRO-ECOLOGY

The Marxist Boomerang

WAS MARX A GROWTH FREAK?

Marx thought you could fight capitalism by allowing it to grow, thus creating a strong class of industrial workers who would eventually 'break their chains' by kicking out the owners and taking over production themselves. He called such growth the development of the *productive forces*.

MAINLY TECHNOLOGY AND LABOUR

Most modern technology, however, by plundering nature is in conflict with the *conditions of production*.

NATURAL RESOURCES LIKE RAW MATERIALS, CLIMATE AND BIOLOGICAL FERTILITY

Marx left the impression that natural resources were in principle unlimited – that humanity would always find new ones. In the Communist Manifesto he declared that one of the aims of socialism would be 'to increase the total of productive forces as rapidly as possible'.

NOWADAYS THAT'S A RECIPE FOR ECO-DISASTER

ECO FLO

Ecologists have shown that the very growth Marx saw as a step to revolution – and as a reasonable course after it – can destroy the natural environment on which all economic activity depends.

Some radical ecologists suggest that it's also robbing the workers of their political strength by destroying skill and creativity with meaningless jobs, robots and computers, and dividing them as a class (and offering by way of compensation the idea that the only thing worth striving for is material wealth).

These ecologists argue that not just ownership needs attacking but the whole technocratic structure of modern industrial society, along with the growth myth. 'Growth socialism' can postpone eco-disaster for a while by using technology and resources more efficiently, but the end result will be the same.

A planned economy is a condition for real change. But if it lacks an ecological perspective . . .

Socialism without ecology

Soviet 'socialism' is no different from Western capitalism in its development view, its belief that nature is simply an object to be exploited and that technology can solve all problems.

The result? Nearly 10% of the Soviet Union's habitable territory is now sterile land, wasteland or semi-wasteland. It has been mined, dumped, tailed, slagged and sludged, polluted, buried, swamped and burned, deforested, eroded and salinated.

Ecologically, according to a Soviet government official, Siberia may soon be transformed from 'an inexhaustible source of resources' into 'a frozen wasteland that will be harder to revitalise than the burning deserts of Central Asia' (Boris Komarov).

In the Soviet Union, as in the West, environment protection laws go by the board when they obstruct industrial progress. But, unlike in the West, there is no grassroots environment movement to protest.

Soviet nuclear reactors, sold all over Eastern Europe and abroad, lack safety containments and emergency cooling systems.

LIKE A RACING CAR WITHOUT BRAKES

IN THE WEST THEY'D BE BANNED

But the public hears no hint of the risks so there is no public opposition.

SOCIALISM WITHOUT ECOLOGY IS FATAL... ESPECIALLY WHEN IT'S UNDEMOCRATIC

ECO FLO

AND IT EARNS YOU A ROTTEN REPUTATION — JUST LISTEN! ....

An Indian Speaks

Europeans may see (Marxist materialism) as revolutionary but American Indians see it simply as still more of that same old European conflict between being and gaining.

*Being is a spiritual proposition. Gaining is a material act. Traditionally, American Indians have always attempted to be the best people they could. Part of that spiritual process was and is to give away wealth, to discard wealth in order **not to gain**. Material gain is an indicator of false status among traditional people while it is 'proof that the system works' to Europeans ...*

*Most important here is the fact that Europeans feel no sense of loss in all this. After all, their philosophers have despiritualised reality so there is no satisfaction (for them) to be gained in simply observing the wonder of a mountain or a lake or a people **in being**. Satisfaction is measured in terms of gaining material – so the mountain becomes gravel and the lake becomes coolant for a factory ...*

I do not believe that capitalism itself is really responsible for the situation in which (American Indians) have been declared a national sacrifice. No, it is the European tradition. European culture itself is responsible. Marxism is just the latest continuation of this tradition, not a solution to it. There is another way. There is the traditional Lakota way and the ways of the other American Indian peoples. It is the way that knows that humans do not have the right to degrade Mother Earth, that there are forces beyond anything the European mind has conceived, that humans must be in harmony with all relations or the relations will eventually eliminate the disharmony.

All European tradition, Marxism included, has conspired to defy the natural order of all things. Mother Earth has been abused, the powers have been abused, and this cannot go on forever. No theory can alter that simple fact. Mother Earth will retaliate, the whole environment will retaliate, and the abusers will be eliminated. Things come full circle. Back to where it started. That's revolution.

– excerpts from an address by Russell Means at the 1980 Black Hills Alliance Survival Gathering.

DON'T BE TOO HARSH ON MARX – HE DID HIS BIOLOGY

RIGHT FOR EXAMPLE IN DAS KAPITAL I WARNED THAT CAPITALIST PRODUCTION "DISTURBS THE CIRCULATION OF MATTER BETWEEN MAN AND THE SOIL AND PREVENTS THE RETURN TO THE SOIL OF ITS ELEMENTS" – PURE ECOLOGY

The Chinese Marxists under Mao worked as far as possible *with* nature instead of *against* it. They pooled land and labour and built agriculture on their greatest resource, human energy (instead of miracle seed technology), while industry was small- and medium-scale, evenly spread, and employed modern and traditional techniques that conserved resources and minimised waste.

With the commune as the basic unit and the party as an effective instrument of administration, the Chinese stressed cooperation and self-reliance and became a model for alternative development in the Third World.

AHH, THOSE WERE THE DAYS

BUT NOW WE'RE MOVING IN ANOTHER DIRECTION

COMPETE MORE

LET'S TRY TO PIN-DOWN ECOLOGY

AND SEE WHERE IT COMES INTO THE PICTURE

Ecology is more than just a branch of biology. It brings together a string of natural and social sciences, as well as philosophy, and studies nature *as a whole*. This 'holistic' approach is what makes it such a broad subject. Its central theme is the interdependence of all living things.

EKOLOGY SKOOL

ENERGY
GENETICS
PHYSICS
HISTORY
TECHNOLOGY
ANTHROPOLOGY
EVOLUTION
ECONOMICS
BIOLOGY
ECOLOGY
PHILOSOPHY
POLITICS
POPULATION
ETC.
CHEMISTRY
ETC.

Ideas about ecology cropped up in the 18th century, when the industrial capitalists were breaking out of their ecological niches and founding empires.

Science had just broken out of *its* traditional niche – the pursuit of wisdom for human enlightenment and perfection – and adopted the idea that humanity's proper role on Earth was to extend its power over nature as far as possible.

NATURE IS A MACHINE

AND TECHNOLOGY THE TOOL-KIT

IMPERIALIST MANIPULATORS THE PAIR OF YOU

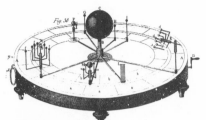

This 'mechanical' model of nature has dominated Western thinking ever since, and served capitalism well. It has also shaped the development of ecology. Some modern ecologists call their field 'bio-economics' . . . nature is transformed into a business division.

Of course there have been ecologists who didn't fit in, who insisted that humanity could never be an island unto itself.

I'M FOR PEACEFUL CO-EXISTENCE WITH NATURE

Gilbert White, English Curate, 1720 - 1793

ALL IS ONE AND INTER-RELATED

Henry David Thoreau, American Naturalist 1817 - 1862

The 20th century brought a growing number of 'misfits'. At first their views made little impact on the owners and planners of industrial society or on the public consciousness. But then . . .

123

The Age of Ecology

Smack in the middle of the West's Second Industrial Revolution a 1962 book by an American nature writer, Rachel Carson's Silent Spring, created a sensation. It showed how the new biocides flooding the environment were a threat to humanity on a par with nuclear war. Carson shared White's and Thoreau's vision of the unity of all life and urged scientists to take a humbler approach to nature.

WE MUST REALISE WE ARE ONLY A TINY PART OF A VAST AND INCREDIBLE UNIVERSE

The book launched the modern ecology movement and the fires were fuelled by another American biologist, Barry Commoner, who analysed the explosive increase of pollution and found the ecological chains were being broken by capitalism's new production techniques and its replacement of natural products by synthetics.

PRODUCTION FOR PROFIT TENDS TO BE HIGHLY DESTRUCTIVE

By the 1970s the message was loud and unmistakable – there were indeed limits to growth. Graphs showed population and pollution soaring and resources dwindling, and somewhere in the mid-21st century the collapse of the industrial base, taking with it the agricultural and service sectors. Suddenly, the ecologists had everyone's ear . . . well, almost . . .

The environment lobby swelled from a small community of experts into a mass movement around the world, well-informed and many-sided. People of all shapes, sizes and political hues became active, directing their main effort at the nuclear threat but also engaging in a wide variety of local actions that pointed towards a more human environment and satisfying lifestyle.

By the 1980s, as bottled freshwater began selling well in the shops and the microchip promised to change the face of industrial society, the science of ecology was firmly rooted at the centre of any serious discussion about desirable futures.

Ecology without socialism

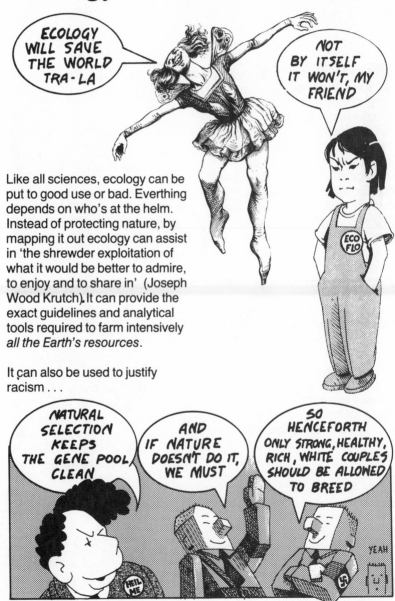

Like all sciences, ecology can be put to good use or bad. Everthing depends on who's at the helm. Instead of protecting nature, by mapping it out ecology can assist in 'the shrewder exploitation of what it would be better to admire, to enjoy and to share in' (Joseph Wood Krutch). It can provide the exact guidelines and analytical tools required to farm intensively *all the Earth's resources*.

It can also be used to justify racism . . .

. . . or to confuse the issue and cement inequality.

WE'RE ALL IN THE SAME BOAT

Understanding the way nature works is vitally important. Ecology can establish what we can and cannot do if the 'web of life' is to be kept intact, and it can be used to radically criticise society. But in itself it is only a tool.

To decide how it should be used means choosing between different lifestyles, systems and types of civilisation.

AND THAT FOLKS IS A POLITICAL CHOICE

Choosing

THESE ARE THE ALTERNATIVES AS ILLICH SEES THEM

Either we agree to impose limits on technology and industrial production so as to conserve natural resources, preserve the ecological balances necessary to life, and favour the development and autonomy of communities and individuals . . .

HE CALLS THIS **CONVIVIAL** SOCIETY

. . . or else the limits necessary to the preservation of life will be centrally determined and planned by ecological engineers, and the programmed production of an 'optimal environment' will be entrusted to centralised institutions and hard technologies.

HE CALLS THAT THE TECHNO-FASCIST PATH

AND IN HIS OPINION WE'RE HALFWAY DOWN IT ALREADY

futures

Technology is supposed to provide for human needs. But its main function has been to substitute non-human energy and machines for people.

SOMETIMES THATS GOOD

KICK

BUT OFTEN IT MEANS BOREDOM OR UNEMPLOYMENT

Capitalism has developed the kind of technology that serves its interests, and ignored or obstructed techniques that do not. This has usually resulted in technology that is destructive of nature. Consequently, brilliant scientists are now spending whole careers trying to 'copy' nature and create artificial life in laboratories.

WE'VE ALREADY CLONED THE CARROT

AND WE'VE SYNTHESISED SUGAR

TATE LYLE

sunlight UNILEVER

WONDER WHERE THIS IS ALL LEADING?

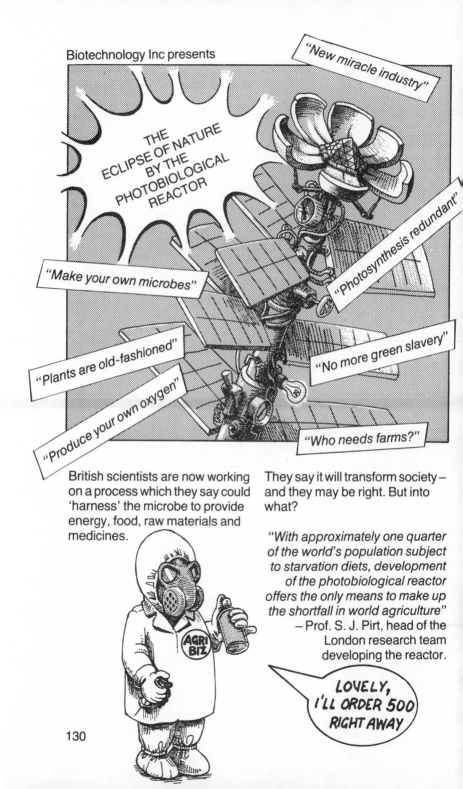

Biotechnology Inc presents

THE ECLIPSE OF NATURE BY THE PHOTOBIOLOGICAL REACTOR

"New miracle industry"

"Photosynthesis redundant"

"Make your own microbes"

"No more green slavery"

"Plants are old-fashioned"

"Produce your own oxygen"

"Who needs farms?"

British scientists are now working on a process which they say could 'harness' the microbe to provide energy, food, raw materials and medicines.

They say it will transform society – and they may be right. But into what?

"With approximately one quarter of the world's population subject to starvation diets, development of the photobiological reactor offers the only means to make up the shortfall in world agriculture" – Prof. S. J. Pirt, head of the London research team developing the reactor.

LOVELY, I'LL ORDER 500 RIGHT AWAY

Air pollution and noise monitor in Tokyo

Are we sure that we want to 'escape the limitations of conventional agriculture'? Is that the best way? Do we really want the freedom of the astronaut: freedom from natural food and drink, natural surroundings, freedom to regard the Earth as an object?

Who decides? Who, if anyone, is taking the responsibility? Unless technology is brought under social control it will go its own way, manipulated by power-groups for short-term gain, and decide our future for us.

Radical eco-solutions

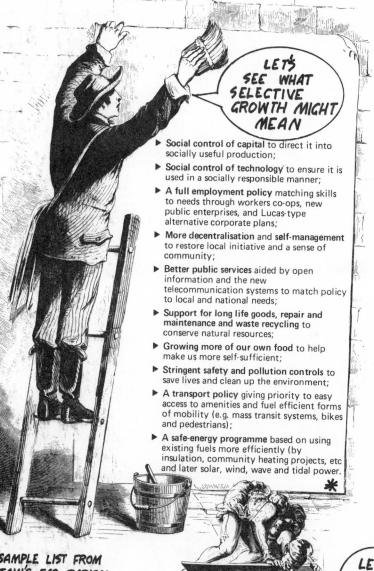

LET'S SEE WHAT SELECTIVE GROWTH MIGHT MEAN

▶ **Social control of capital** to direct it into socially useful production;

▶ **Social control of technology** to ensure it is used in a socially responsible manner;

▶ **A full employment policy** matching skills to needs through workers co-ops, new public enterprises, and Lucas-type alternative corporate plans;

▶ **More decentralisation** and **self-management** to restore local initiative and a sense of community;

▶ **Better public services** aided by open information and the new telecommunication systems to match policy to local and national needs;

▶ **Support for long life goods, repair and maintenance and waste recycling** to conserve natural resources;

▶ **Growing more of our own food** to help make us more self-sufficient;

▶ **Stringent safety and pollution controls** to save lives and clean up the environment;

▶ **A transport policy** giving priority to easy access to amenities and fuel efficient forms of mobility (e.g. mass transit systems, bikes and pedestrians);

▶ **A safe-energy programme** based on using existing fuels more efficiently (by insulation, community heating projects, etc and later solar, wind, wave and tidal power.

＊A SAMPLE LIST FROM BRITAIN'S ECO-RADICAL GROUP - **SERA**

LET'S HAVE A CLOSER LOOK

SELECTIVE GROWTH

Goods must be good

LET'S WORK LESS, BETTER AND DIFFERENTLY

The French ecologist André Gorz says unemployment in the rich countries suggests that less time is now required to produce the *necessities* of life.

IF EVERYONE WORKED LESS WE COULD HAVE FULL EMPLOYMENT

RIGHT TO WORK

Gorz argues that we can live better by working and consuming less – as long as we produce good quality, durable things that are not harmful and do not create resource scarcity when generally available. In fact, the only things *worth* producing are those which remain good for everyone when everyone has access to them . . . things which do not create privilege for some at the expense of others.

FRESH FOOD?

TRAINS? POWER TOOLS? HI-FI?

FAIR-PRICED HOUSING?

BIKES? TOUGH SHOES?

POCKET CALCULATO?

To escape the eco-crisis and beat technofascism, says Gorz, we must *redirect* production instead of increasing it, making other things in other ways.

Wage-labour production would meet society's basic needs while 'informal' production – people doing work for themselves, swapping with friends and neighbours, etc – would provide a vast array of goods and services over and above the necessities.

Also, says Gorz, it would help us to move away from the division of labour and allow us to choose different levels of consumption and different lifestyles.

Near & Far

Decentralisation makes it easier for people to produce what they consume and consume what they produce. Local production makes sense for a lot of things.

Insofar as the natural resources exist locally transport is saved and therefore energy as well. Food is a good example. Instead of freighting bread, grain, meat and vegetables up and down the country or importing them . . .

Big & Small

But local production isn't always possible – or desirable. Certain raw materials are only to be found in certain areas. And a lot of machinery & parts demand highly specialised and expensive equipment.

Large-scale *can* provide better goods or work safety. Some things cannot be or should not be decentralised or scaled down.

Resources must be shared, locally, regionally, nationally and internationally, producing things that others need as well as for ourselves.

A human environment

Norway's political ecologists distinguish between *complex systems* and *complicated systems* when seeking to outline suitable living environments for human beings.

WHERE COMPLEX MEANS DIVERSE

AND COMPLICATED MEANS, HARD TO DEAL WITH

Complex systems
Little dependence on outside world
Self-defined activity
Integrated work
Overall view
Co-determination, responsibility
Symmetrical relationships (mutual exchange)
Cooperation between equals
Local diversity
Majority working in small units
Limited transport needs

THIS MODEL ENCOURAGES SELF·RELIANCE

Complicated systems
Great dependence on outside world
Most activity defined by others
Division of labour
Confusion due to fragmentary, misleading information
Alienation
One-sided relationships (adjustment, exploitation)
Hierarchical relationships, competition
Specialisation
Large units dominate
Extensive transport needs

Ecological planning

Davis, a Californian town of 35,000 inhabitants, was the first in the US to adopt an Energy Conservation Building Code. This led to ecologically sound planning policies which changed the face of the town.

Today, Davis is a prime example of how living standards can be raised without damaging the environment. Ecological planning in Davis means conservation of energy, water and farmland and a high degree of self-sufficiency.

A typical neighbourhood unit, managed by its inhabitants, holds monthly meetings in the community building to discuss problems and plan improvements. Junior schools, shops, post offices and green zones are within walking distance.

New-built district centres provide a bakery, medical practice, restaurant, 'fix-it-yourself' workshop and a food co-op which in principle sells one product of each sort, chosen by the local inhabitants.

140

The whole town is linked by a cycle network, complete with signposts, toilets and drinking fountains.

SO 25% OF ALL TRANSPORT HERE IS BY BIKE

Roads are narrow (so small, low-energy cars are preferred) and do not run through living areas. Public transport is well developed.

THEY'VE EVEN BOUGHT LONDON DOUBLE-DECKERS

50% OF OUR OPEN GROUND IS CULTIVATED

MEETING 25% OF OUR NEEDS

Almost everthing planted in Davis is edible – fruit trees, berry bushes, etc – and each district has a communal compost heap.

I PASS ON PRACTICAL TIPS AND INFORMATION

UNDER THE SUN

MOST NEW BUILDINGS ARE SOLAR HEATED

WE RECYCLE EVERYTHING FROM PAPER TO MOTOR OIL

RECYCLING TRUCK

WONDER IF WE CAN SURVIVE THE REAGAN ADMINISTRATION?

Ecological farming

Modern 'industrial' farming, with its monoculture and biocides, energy-guzzling machinery and fertiliser, cannot feed us in the long run. There are other ways that can . . .

TO GOVERNMENT agronomists, organic farming is a scandalous state of affairs, an incredible step backwards. Think of it: "Farming with manure! It's like going back to the time of Louis XIV!"

In the face of such criticism, Philippe Desbrosses, vice-president of the Federation Nationale d'Agriculture Biologique (FNAB), one of France's biggest organic farming groups, simply gives a Gallic shrug. His farm, near Romorantin in the Loir-et-Cher departement, has been officially recognised as best in the region.

Guardian Weekly 31·08·81

VIVE LA BIOLOGIE!

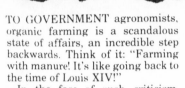

CHEMICALS

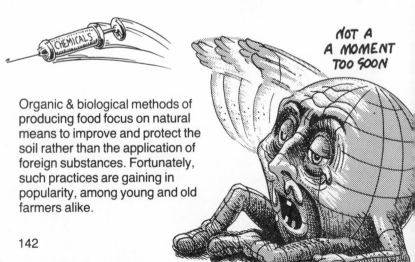

NOT A A MOMENT TOO SOON

Organic & biological methods of producing food focus on natural means to improve and protect the soil rather than the application of foreign substances. Fortunately, such practices are gaining in popularity, among young and old farmers alike.

A US government survey showed
that in 1980 over 26,000 farmers
in 23 states were using organic
methods, on farms of all sizes.
Most were selling their produce
for the same price as the
conventional farmer.

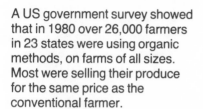

AND OUR CROPS WERE USUALLY AS LARGE

BUT WE HAD WITHDRANAL SYMPTOMS TO START WITH

The switch from chemical farming
to organic or biological isn't easy,
especially if the farm has been
without livestock for a long time.

Many of the US farmers had three
or four difficult years before the
soil could be restored to natural
life.

BUT THEN THINGS QUICKLY GOT GOING

143

In contrast to the Agribusinessman the ecologically-minded farmer is a first-rate technician. He or she masters the demanding technique of creating new and sustainable ecosystems through which life-energy can flow freely and naturally. This requires a thorough understanding of how nature works. For example, you need to know . . .

An alternative farming policy would stress not only sound soil practices but also self-reliance and a radically different overall structure.

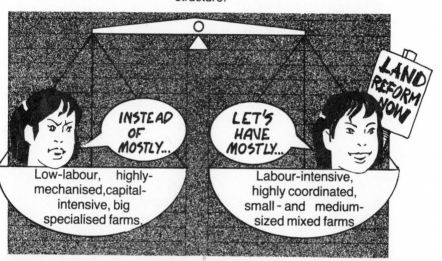

Cleaner & Safer

The sooner we force governments to switch from nuclear power and fossil fuels to energy from the sun, wind, water and biomass, the quicker we can stop pollution and ease the threat to world peace.

Forcing governments to stop producing weapons of mass destruction — the worst pollutants of all — would release funds for the giant task of removing the toxic elements now poisoning the biosphere.

Recycling

One way to save energy is to take a leaf out of nature's book and keep everything going round and round.

Paper, scrap metals and glass should also be recycled. Even plastic can be re-used.

People's Technology

Does the future really belong to Flash Gordon? Many scientists and technicians around the world, amateur and professional, are pursuing a path *away* from technofascism. Appropriate . . . soft . . . intermediate . . . alternative . . . convivial . . . radical . . . whatever their technologies are called they share some common features.

WE'RE NOT AGAINST TECHNOLOGY - WE'RE FASCINATED BY IT

ECOLOGICALLY ACCEPTABLE TECHNIQUES

COMBINING OLD AND NEW

ENCOURAGING LOCAL USE AND DEMOCRACY

INSTEAD OF CENTRALISM AND TECHNOCRACY

'Advanced' technology usually means supertankers, missiles, breeders, etc. But what could be more advanced than using technology not just to spare labour but to decentralise and equip society on a human scale for human needs? It's a job with a future . . .

WE CAN NOW DESIGN THE MACHINERY FOR ELIMINATING SLAVERY WITHOUT ENSLAVING MAN TO THE MACHINE

We have vacancies for radical technologists in the fields of transport, work safety, energy systems, waste management, fibre research, food production, environmental control, housebuilding, agriculture, forestry, textiles, electronics, metallurgy, furniture-making, machine design, cybernetics and just about any other field you care to name except mass destruction!

THEY COULD MAKE VIRTUALLY INDESTRUCTIBLE TEXTILES

WORKER CONTROLLED TECHNOLOGY

AND EASILY REPAIRED MACHINES GOOD FOR 50 OR 100 YEARS

NOT TECHNOLOGY CONTROLLED WORKERS

An alternative society in solidarity with the Third World would seek to help the poorer countries with things the people there need most — cheap, labour-saving and fuel-saving technology appropriate to village conditions and small-scale cooperative industries, carefully-researched and field-tested.

LIKE GOOD STOVES, GRINDERS, PUMPS AND LOOMS

BETTER LATHES AND PRESSES

149

Solidarity

If the Earth's resources belong to us all is there a way of sharing them out fairly?

> **WITHOUT INTERNATIONAL SOCIALISM? — I DOUBT IT**

Karl Marx

The 'ecological perspective' implies global solidarity — that we're all responsible for everyone alive today, for future generations, and for the Earth, which is our common home.

It implies a drastic restructuring of production and consumption patterns to ensure a decent life for the large section of humanity whose basic needs are not being met.

It implies a different set of values — that we must stop measuring people by their 'efficiency' and 'productivity' and start talking about health, harmony, beauty, justice and equality.

> **AND LOVE**

ECO JOE

But such a society will remain a vision unless we break the hold of the Power Machine . . .

150

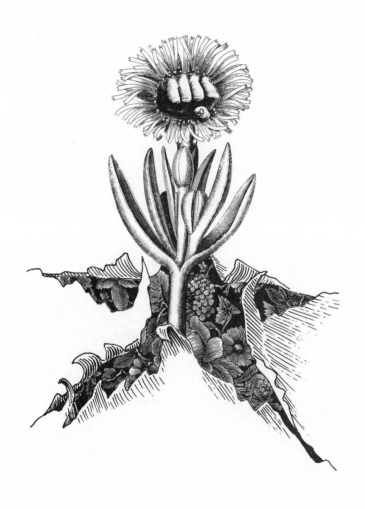

Struggle!

THERE'S NO REASON FOR OPTIMISM

THERE'S NO REASON FOR PESSIMISM

THERE'S EVERY REASON TO ACT NOW

The present economic system may be rigid, but the people running it are neither stupid nor unimaginative. They specialise in absorbing protest and ripping off progressive ideas, and they will always try to adapt ecological demands to their own ends.

HMM...

THERE'S A GREAT FUTURE FOR CLONED VEGETABLES

I CONTROL 300,000 LITTLE COMPUTER-LINKED ENTERPRISES

ALTERNATIVE FOOD INC.

SMALL SCALE (WORLDWIDE) INC

It's the technofascist vision that will become reality unless monopoly capitalism and state bureaucracies are fought *politically*. The various alternatives, however subversive, will be islands of sanity in a sea of madness as long as we do nothing about the competitive system that is degrading most people's lives.

Sometimes it's hard to separate
environment-conscious people in
the labour movement . . .

. . . from politically-conscious
people in the environment
movement . . .

... while the poor are organising ...

... and the traditional peoples are also resisting.

And as for the consumers . . .

Is what I make at work really useful or necessary?
Can it be made better?
Is there a shortage of goods or services anywhere that my workplace could meet?
How could our production be reorganised?
Does my working environment need improving?
Can the work itself be made more enjoyable?
Is my union interested in these questions?
Is my party doing anything about the environment?
Is my environment group on the right track?
Can I cycle to work instead?
Can I start a car pool with friends, neighbours, workmates?
Do I really need all the things I buy?
Do they waste resources or damage the environment?
Do they benefit Agribiz?
Do they deprive the Third World?
Is there local produce I can buy instead?
Can I help start a local co-op?
Can I help draw up a shopping list for 'alternative consumers'?
Is there an allotment or a patch of land I could cultivate?
Where can I find out more?

Eco-demands

§ Let human needs and
ecological care shape
production and lifestyles!

§ Meaningful work, a
reasonable living standard
and a clean environment for
all!

§ Conservation of energy and
raw materials!

Three Radicals to Read...

BILLY THE BOOKWORM SAYS :-

YIPPEE!

Bahro's

Rudolf Bahro is an East German Marxist who was jailed for criticising the brand of socialism officially practised inside the Soviet bloc. After international protests he was released to the West in 1979 and became a leading figure in the ecology coalition in West Germany *Die Grünen* (The Greens), while remaining a committed socialist. In his book, 'The Alternative', which led to his imprisonment, Bahro shows how East Europe's 'non-capitalist' road to industrialisation has been shaped by the same growth ideals and methods as has Western capitalism. He also shows how the working classes of both West and East have the exploitation of nature and the Third World in common. Defending their own societies' privileged positions on the world market, they add to global inequality.

Historical Compromise

Bahro identifies monopoly capitalism's constant search for new profits as the major cause of the environment crisis threatening humanity. But the Left must revise its traditional thinking about strategies for change. To achieve a democratic, participatory form of socialism requires an 'historical compromise' linking the labour movement with what Bahro calls the new social movements – the environment movement, women's movement, peace movement and alternative projects. People are fighting the system in many different ways and because resistance is cutting across class and party lines a grand coalition of anti-capitalist forces is needed to unite them.

Bahro views the division of labour as the key to oppression at work and at home, and examines ways of breaking it down and rebuilding society from the bottom upwards, starting from self-governing neighbourhoods and workplaces and a network of 'free communes'.

The Alternative: towards a critique of real, existing socialism. New Left Books, London, 1979.

Illich's

Ivan Illich, one of the world's foremost social thinkers, based in Mexico, says he is trying to show 'that two-thirds of mankind can still avoid passing through the industrial age, by choosing right now a post-industrial balance in their mode of production which the hyper-industrial nations will be forced to adopt as an alternative to chaos.'

Illich has written a series of books criticising modern society and its failure to cater to human needs. The privileged today, he says, are not those who consume most but those who can escape the negative byproducts of industrialisation – people who can commute outside the rush hour, be born or die at home, cure themselves when ill, breathe fresh air and build their own dwellings. The under-privileged are those who are forced to seek satisfaction through *having* instead of *doing*, to consume the 'packaged goods and services designed and prescribed by professionals'. People must fight this new priesthood of specialists and experts. They must arm themselves with the self-confidence and the means to run their own lives as far as possible, especially as big institutions like schooling, medical care and transport today are creating more problems than they solve.

Vernacular Conviviality

Politics, says Illich, is no longer a simple Left-Right choice. Now we must also choose between 'soft' and 'hard' (energy, technology, etc.) and between what he calls in his latest works 'vernacular' values and 'industrial' ones. This is a variation on the 'conviviality' versus 'technofascism' theme but Illich is very precise about definitions and says 'vernacular' is the closest he can get to naming 'those acts of competence, lust or concern that we want to defend from measurement or manipulation by Chicago Boys and Socialist Commissars'.

Tools for Conviviality, 1973, *The Right to Useful Unemployment and its Professional Enemies*, 1978, *Shadow Work*, 1981. All published by Boyars, London.

soft

left

industrial

vernacular

right

hard

Gorz's

André Gorz is an author and journalist living in Paris, where he writes for *Le Nouvel Observateur* under the name of Michel Bosquet. Born in Austria, like Illich, and strongly influenced by him, Gorz is a libertarian socialist Marx, he says, can be found in Illich but Illich can not be found in Marx – except when Marx declares that the 'free development of each is the condition for the free development of all' (Communist Manifesto). Gorz sees the ecology struggle not as an end in itself but as an essential part of the larger struggle against capitalism and technofascism.

Civil Society

Capitalism, he points out, can adapt to ecological constraints. Therefore it's important to keep one's eye on the main goal – 'a social, economic and cultural revolution that abolishes the constraints of capitalism and in so doing establishes a new relationship between the individual and society and between people and nature.'

Gorz champions a 'civil society', shifting power from the State and political parties to the local community and the 'web of social relations that individuals establish amongst themselves'. The State's role would be to spread knowledge and equip the citizens for self-management. In *Ecology as Politics* Gorz analyses why we're experiencing ever-increasing costs and decreasing satisfaction, and how 'we can do more with less'. To free the imagination, he also sketches a utopian future France, with a 20-hour working week, a lively odd-job sector, guaranteed minimum wage for all, environmentally sound forms of production and a cultural life that encourages the development of a rich, all-round personality.

Ecology as Politics, South End Press, Boston, 1980 (UK distributor Pluto Press)

Some more books

Easy-to-read introductions to the environment issue include **The Closing Circle**, by Barry Commoner (Alfred A. Knopf, h/c; Bantam, p/b), which makes the political connections.

Nature's Economy, by Donald Worster (Doubleday Anchor), is a history of ecology.

Future alternatives are examined in **The Self-Managing Environment**, by Alan Roberts (Rowman); **Stepping Stones: Appropriate Technology and Beyond**, edited by Lane DeMoll and Gigi Cole (Schocken); **Eco-Philosophy**, by Henryk Skolimowski (Boyars—Merrimack Book Service); and **Political Ecology: An Activist's Reader**, by Alexander Cockburn and James Ridgeway (Times Books). **Europe 2000**, edited by Peter Hall (Columbia University Press), is the result of an eight-year international study on how Europe will look if it adapts to environmental and resource constraints.

The Third World situation is best analysed in **Food First**, by Frances M. Lappe and Joseph Collins (Ballantine), and **Beyond the Green Revolution**, by Kenneth Dahberg (Plenum Press). **The Famine Business**, by Colin Tudge (St. Martin's Press),also looks at food politics in general.

Who Owns the Earth?, by James Ridgeway (Macmillan), details ownership of resources, and **The Pesticide Conspiracy**, by Robert Van Den Bosch (Doubleday Anchor), pits the ecologist against Big Business.

All farmers should read **Radical Agriculture**, edited by Richard Merrill (Harper and Row), and all city-dwellers need **The Complete Urban Farmer**, by David Wickers (Penguin).

The Destruction of Nature in the Soviet Union, by Boris Komarov (M. E. Sharpe), shows the need for eco-socialism in the USSR.

Taking Action

All these groups are active in environmental issues:

The National Audubon Society
950 Third Avenue
New York City 10022

The Sierra Club
530 Bush Street
San Francisco, CA 94108

The Wilderness Society
1901 Pennsylvania Avenue NW
Washington, D.C. 20006

The Environmental Defense Fund
1525 18th Street NW
Washington, D.C. 20036

The National Resource Defense Council
1725 I Street NW
Suite 600
Washington, D.C. 20006

The Solar Lobby
1001 Connecticut Avenue NW
Suite 510
Washington, D.C. 20036

The Environmental Policy Center
317 Pennsylvania Avenue SE
Washington, D.C. 20003

The Defenders of Wildlife
1244 19th Street NW
Washington, D.C. 20036

Acknowledgements

We drew material from all of the books mentioned, especially those of Bahro, Dahlberg, Dasmann, Gorz, Harrison, Illich, Judge and Worster. Stan Rosenthal and Per Janse made a notable impact and thanks are also due to John Lorraine, Erik Lindfeldt, Kaianders and the Växjö Connection, Peter, Jonas, Sämjan and Vemjan, Ann Sofie-Olbers and last but not least Karin Sperlings.

Steve   William

Picture Credits
Wolf Krabel   p 91, 99
Peter Solbjerghøj   p 101
Pressens Bild   p 89, 95

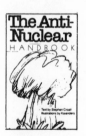